Crystal Set Building and More:
The Xtal Set Society Newsletter Volume 6 and 7

Crystal Set Building and More:
The Xtal Set Society Newsletter Volume 6 and 7

 The Xtal Set Society

Printed in the United States of America
ISBN: 1-887736-09-3

Thank you to all the members of the Xtal Set Society for your enthusiasm and dedication. A special thanks to the members who contributed to this compilation, in order of appearance: Edward Richley, William Simes, Alan Klase, Robert Rowe, Nile Steiner, Larry Hall, Bob Flick, Jim Penland, P.A. Kinzie, John Franke, Joseph Cooper, George Trudeau.

Welcome to the Xtal Set Society

Crystal Set Radios? Yes, that's right. Over 90 years since their invention, Xtal Sets are still capturing people's attention. The Xtal Set Society was founded in 1991 and is dedicated to building and experimenting with crystal set radios. When I was first asked to run the Society, I wasn't sure how many folks still liked building these little sets, but I soon found out that Xtal sets have a following all over the globe. We've been getting faxes and e-mails from around the world at all times of the day and night saying, "Who the heck are you guys? Can I get more information?" One customer e-mailed us from our web page, "I was so flabbergasted to find a society of Xtal set builders that I fell off my chair." This theme seems to reoccur throughout our mail as Xtal set builders are joyous to find a home while still not quite believing it, "You mean there are others out there like me? A whole society?" Another customer, after receiving our newsletter, presented it to his wife and exclaimed, "See, it's not just me!" Our members include engineers, electronics enthusiasts, amateur radio operators, antique radio buffs, science teachers, and many others.

Every other month the Society publishes a newsletter with projects and articles sent in by our members. This compilation contains all issues from January 1996 through November 1997. Our newsletters are packed full of projects and information about Crystal Radios, mostly dealing with design and electronics issues. You'll also find a few TRF sets and one tubers; we focus on simple, old-time, elegant radio circuits that enthusiasts can build from scratch. Members are encouraged to send projects and information into the Society and to correspond with each other. For more information please see the back of this book.

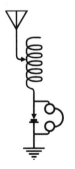

Rebecca Hewes, Editor
The Xtal Set Society, 1998

Table of Contents

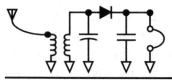

The Xtal Set Society Newsletter

| Volume 6, No. 1 | January 1, 1996 |

IN THIS ISSUE (#28)—January 1, 1996

AN FM XTAL SET
by Edward Richley

From the Editor's Desk: Ed expressed interest in designing a passive FM crystal set some time ago, prompted by membership discussions in this newsletter, and we received a paper describing Ed's design on November 6th. Due to its length and complexity, we've decided to split its presentation into two parts: theory first and then schematic, construction, and operation in the next issue. This project will require some head scratching and study by members but we accept the challenge! Additional basic theory on FM can be found in The ARRL Handbook. Ed says, "This project requires not only some mechanical skill, but also some RF expertise...more than most crystal sets." An FM set, while not historic, is still a crystal set because Ed shows us how to detect and listen to FM by using the power of the FM signal itself...and after all, isn't that a crystal set!

From an historical point of view, it makes no sense to build a passive receiver for frequency modulation. By the time FM was developed, electronics had become an established technology. However, building unusual circuits can be a lot of fun.

Just as an AM Xtal receiver is just an AM detector with tuning and matching, an FM Xtal set can be built around an FM detector.

Although we are taught that there are several different types of FM detectors, the similarities between the various designs are undeniable. In fact, they can all be classified as quadrature detectors. Although Armstrong would have objected to my saying so, as he spent much effort contesting this issue, at the core of all FM detector designs lies the principle of quadrature detection. Hence, an FM Xtal set consists of the usual crystal set tuned circuit - for matching, and a quadrature detector. In FM reception, the goal is to convert small frequency deviations into an audio signal. As we shall see, the key concept is that by converting these small frequency deviations into phase deviations, the audio signal can be easily extracted.

The basic diagram of a quadrature detector is shown in Figure 1. Signals from the input (the antenna in this case), are split into two roughly equal signals by a wideband power splitter (either 0 degree or 180 degree). The term "wideband" is meant to imply that the relative phase shift between X and Y, whatever its nominal value, doesn't change much with frequency. In other words, the power splitter doesn't contain any resonant circuits (that would mess up splitting the signal.)

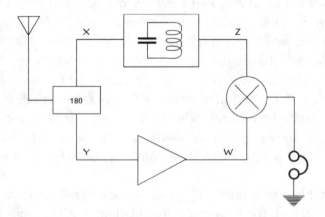

Figure 1: Block diagram of a passive quadrature detector

Signal Y then passes through the funny triangular device. The triangular device is another wideband circuit (no resonances) which doesn't substantially affect the phase shift of W with respect to Y. In

12

some circuits, W and Y are connected by a wire (a very wideband device!). In our circuit, the funny triangular device will be a small step-up transformer.

Meanwhile, signal X has a more interesting route. X passes through a resonator. Hopefully, this is the only resonator in the circuit. We are most familiar with resonators, such as the LC "tank" circuit, as devices for filtering. That is, we most commonly think of tuned circuits in terms of their amplitude response. However, one other feature of these wonderful contrivances is that while their amplitude response is at its peak, their phase shift variation with frequency reaches a maximum.

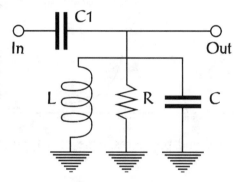

Figure 2: Typical LC resonator

This last point must be understood in order to comprehend how a quadrature detector really operates. Figure 2 shows the familiar LC tank circuit, and the resonant frequency, fo, is calculated as follows:

$$f_o = \frac{1}{2\pi\sqrt{L(C+C1)}}$$

As usual the response of this circuit depends on the "Q," where $Q = \frac{R}{2\pi f_o L}$. Figure 3 shows the familiar amplitude response of the circuit for Q = 500. Note how the response peaks in a very small range of frequency near the resonant frequency. The amplitude of

13

this peak is approximately Q. Furthermore, the bandwidth of the response is approximately f_0/Q.

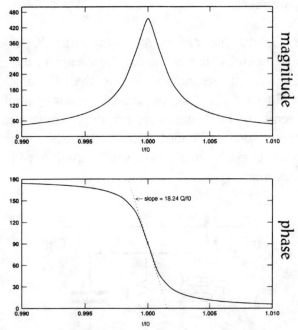

Figure 3: Amplitude and phase response of a typical LC resonator with Q=500.

Meanwhile, the phase between input and output is shown in Figure 3. Incredibly, the phase shift varies considerably within this same bandwidth. In fact, the slope of the phase shift curve, which describes how much the phase changes for a given frequency shift, is roughly $18.25Q/f_0$ near resonance. Thus, the slope is proportional to Q. Note that this large slope occurs while the amplitude response is at its maximum. Also, note that the nominal phase shift at resonance is 90 degrees. This is the reason for the term quadrature detector.

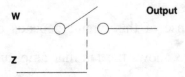

Figure 4: Conceptual operation of a phase detector. Signal Z closes the switch for a short time near its peaks.

Now we have two signals, "Z" and "W." W is a nice signal whose amplitude and phase don't change much with frequency, while Z has large amplitude and large phase shift variations when the resonator is tuned to the incoming carrier. By a suitable non-linear element known as a "phase detector," (don't worry, it's just two diodes), we can convert the phase shifts of Z, with respect to those of W into an audible signal. As you may have guessed, the big circle with the "X" in Figure 1 is the phase detector.

Some readers may already be familiar with balanced modulators. Phase detectors are really the same thing as balanced modulators. Figure 4 shows how a signal "Z" can be used to sample signal "W" at the peaks of Z. The dots in Figure 5 show the sampling of W. When W and Z are in quadrature (90 degrees out of phase), the sampling is zero. When the relative phase changes, the output correspondingly changes. In Figure 4, the phase of Z starts changing at 30 nsec. Before that point, the sampled points are all zero. Afterwards, they start changing. We've already shown how to make phase changes correspond to frequency changes. Thus, by using a resonator and a phase detector, we can produce an output which corresponds to the frequency changes of the input. We can detect FM!

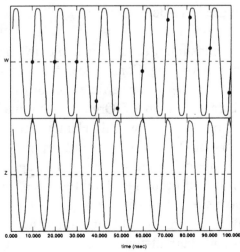

Figure 5: Plot of signal W as sampled at the peaks of signal Z.

15

In practice, the phase detector is not a perfect sampling switch, as implied by Figure 4. It is usually implemented with diodes, and is more like a voltage dependent resistance than a perfect switch. The resistance varies from lower values at the peaks of the control signal to higher values at the valleys. So, it's a really bad switch, but the analogy is nonetheless useful. As long as Z can "connect" W to the output more at its peaks than at other times, the detection can take place.

Editor: That's the theory background for Ed's FM crystal set. Next time, we'll present the design: a high-Q coaxial resonator, fashioned from a 29.5" piece of 2" copper pipe; non-resonant matching circuits, made from readily available TV baluns; and, of course, a couple of 1N34 or similar diodes!

A PICKLE DETECTOR?
By Phil Anderson, WØXI

Did you know that if you wire a dill pickle to 110V AC that it will, after about 20 seconds, light up? I've demonstrated this at a number of amateur radio seminars over the last few years. So, naturally, while editing this edition of the newsletter, I am wondering if the pickle can also be used as a detector? Hm?

A month after demonstrating "burning a pickle" last year at the ARRL Computer Networking Conference, a friend of mine, Phil, KA9Q, sent me a copy of an article he downloaded off the INTERNET, "Characterization of Organic Illumination systems," WRL Technical Note TN-13, by Bill Hamburgen, et al, Western Research Laboratory of Digital Equipment Corporation (DEC), Palo Alto, CA. This got me going on this crazy stuff again! Here's Bill's abstract for the article. "Recent anecdotal reports of novel principles of illumination have stressed qualitative aspects. This note presents a quantitative study of an organic illumination system, characterizing the temperature and current-flow properties of the system as functions of time and device parameters." WOW!

They report that their experiments indicate that pickles are a form of incandescent lamp. Bok Choy, Cornichon, Koshir pickle and Dill pickle emitted light, but a Mandarin Orange did not. In each case the unit under test started at room temperature, heated to over 100 degrees C after ten seconds (except the orange), and then cooled somewhat. Far and away, the pickles offered the least resistance: current at ten seconds was 4.83 amperes for the Kosher and 5.6 for the Dill.

I have no idea where to start to see if we could obtain rectification from such a device. Of course, we'd have to wait about ten to twenty seconds after placing each new specimen into service and we'd have to replace the pickle detector about every minute or so. That's not too practical for listening to a complete program of "The Shadow."

For more "illumination" on this and if you're on the INTERNET, consider downloading a copy of WRL Tech Note TN-13 from WRL-Techreports@decwrl.dec.com.

TIDBITS

Iron pyrites. P.A. Kinzie, Kingman, AZ. Phil mentioned in some notes he sent me that iron pyrites is not quite as sensitive as galena for broadcast detection but is the preferred choice for short wave receivers. Does anybody know why? Does it have to do with the ability of the crystal to react fast enough? Phil?

Buzzers. Earl Thorne, W7HU, Portland OR. Earl sent us a note that reminds us of one of the uses, and perhaps the primary one, of the buzzer with early sets: finding that sensitive spot on the crystal. Here's a quote from Henley's "222 Radio Circuit Designs," first published in 1923, page 68. "In order to test the sensitivity of the crystal detector, the (buzzer) switch is closed and the buzzer started. Various adjustments of the crystal are tried until one which produces loudest response from the buzzer is found. This adjustment usually indicates a sensitive spot on the crystal." Earl goes on to say, "Henley's book is one of my best old books, 73s Earl." *[Editor. You can obtain a reprint of Henley's book from Lindsay Publications Inc, PO BOX 12, Bradley, IL 60915-0012. Would someone like to write a short note on how buzzers of the 1920s were built and worked?]*

Blue blades. Dick Mackiewicz, Coventry, CT. "The hot spot on a blue blade is supposed to be along the line between where the sharp edge is ground and the blue surface. See the attached drawing."

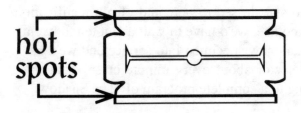

Figure 6: Blue blade

"Cartoon from Radio News, June, 1923. Thanks Dick.

MEMBERSHIP CORRESPONDENCE

Ed Hurd, Palo Alto, CA. "I like to visit the technical library here and look over the English magazine Electronics World/Wireless World which used to be titled just Wireless World. On my last visit I ran across two articles on early detectors: "Coherer-based Radio," July 1994, "Detection Before the Diode," December 1994, and "Detection Before the Diode (again)," January, 1995.

Here's a brief quote from the July article. "Following its introduction a century ago, the coherer electromagnetic wave detector helped radio evolve from being a curiosity to a practical communication tool." Here's a brief quote from the December article. "In the decade before thermionic diodes became widely used for radio reception, the barretter was one of the most popular devices available for rf detection...In 1903, Reginald Fessenden patented the first practical electrolytic detector. He called his detector a barretter—a name apparently derived from the French word for 'exchanger.'"

Scott Thomas, Lexington, KY. Scott sent us some interesting bits and pieces. "My lightning package consists of a spark plug, MOV circuit, and NE2 bulb mounted in a steel box on my ground rod." Guess you don't want to DX lightning anymore Scott? He also sent us an antenna protector schematic shown below. The metal oxide varistor (MOV) limits the voltage to under 170 volts and the chock, L1,cancels out the capacitance of the MOV. Scott! You said you have a spark plug, a gap-type arrestor, in your circuit along side the MOV. Are the two circuits attached in parallel? That would seem logical? *[Editor. MOVs are sometimes called MOV "transient suppressors" and a list of part numbers can be found on page 24.17 of The ARRL Handbook for Radio Amateurs, 1995.]*

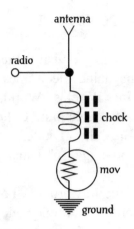

Fig 7: Antenna protector

In addition, Scott asks, "Is there anyone out there selling vari-loopsticks, slug-tuned coils, or 365 μμfd variable caps? These are hard to find! And, has anyone heard of a THERMIONIC IC; one in which tiny tube elements are placed on a chip? I read about this not too long ago but haven't seen anything else?" *[Editor. The tube IC sounds interesting - anyone have leads?]* And in a later note from Scott..."Another indoor antenna is simply a coil wound around a few feet of 1-1/2" PVC and hung vertically taking up little space. Results aren't as good as with a long wire antenna but better than nothing."

Allan Doble, VK3AMD, Australia. "I just read your handbook which was on sale here in Melbourne at Daytronics. I made my first crystal set in 1924 and used it to hear the first broadcast of our national station, 3LO, in Melbourne in 1925. What surprised me was that the handbook did not include a simple circuit that I used to make small crystal sets for friends in the early '30s. It was a trap-tuned set - see the figure below - and the detector was either galena with cat whisker or carborundum. By the way, Dame Nellie Melba sang on the first 3LO broadcast." [Editor. Allan is right. I've not built a trap-tuned set. Maybe it's time. Has anyone else and what were your results?]

20

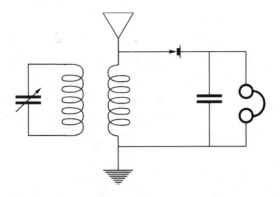

Figure 8: 1930 Trap Tuned Set

Vernon Chappell, San Diego, CA. Vern sent us some hand drawings and notes on various long distance (DX) sets he's made. "For DX, a good aerial and a very good ground are required...The secret of success for high sensitivity is a series-tuned antenna and ground circuit combined with a conventional parallel-tuned tank... the antenna circuit (antenna coil and cap in series) requires more variable capacitance for tuning than the secondary (assuming a 200 foot antenna or there about) ...and one can combine a two-gang variable capacitor (superhet tube type) for that..." Vern says that DXing the 50,000 watt clear channel stations is almost guaranteed. A full-wave detector circuit he used is shown below. "The center-tapped transformer has a 20K primary. The center-tap is grounded, and the 2,000 ohm headphones are wired across the full primary coil." We have no details on coil inductance, part number, etc. An analysis of the circuit would be interesting for various coil inductances.

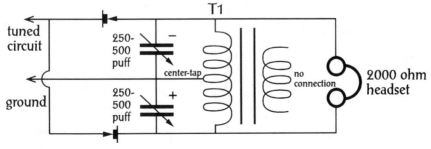

Figure 9: DX detector

K.E. Drews, San Saba, TX. "My first crystal set was a Philmore Little Worlder consisting of a galena xtal and flat coil with spider arm. I ordered it from Allied as a 5th grader for 59 cents in 1937! The first radio I remember as a 4 year old (1929) was one my dad purchased from a farm neighbor, a Crosley Tridyne?. I later found out that that set was based on Armstrong's regenerative patented in 1914."

Frank Jeniker, Lakeside, MT. "I found 'Detectors Made from Rocks,' Volume 5, No. 3 of the newsletter, especially interesting. However, I continue to wonder whether it is the germanium in galena which is the effective agent. Germanium accompanies the lead in its natural ore occurrence."

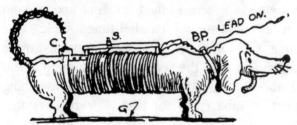

Cartoon from Radio News, June, 1923. Thanks Dick.

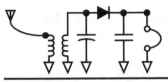

The Xtal Set Society Newsletter

| Volume 6, No. 2 | March 1, 1996 |

IN THIS ISSUE (#29) - March 1, 1996

AN FM XTAL SET (part two of two)
by Edward Richley

From the Editor's Desk: In the January issue, Ed presented his idea for an FM crystal set. He introduced us to the basic concept, presented us with a block diagram, and drew for us an "intuitive" picture of how it all works. In a nutshell, the FM crystal set is nothing more than a quadrature detector and a basic crystal set combined. In this part, Ed fills in the details, showing us how he built what he conceived. The key part, as we'll see, is the high-Q resonator, made from 2 inch copper pipe.

Now that the fundamentals are out of the way, we can go about implementing a receiver for the FM broadcast band, using no active components. A typical superheterodyne receiver will convert an FM carrier frequency to a lower intermediate frequency (IF), and build selectivity into the set at the IF. This makes the superhet more complex but simplifies the filtering, allowing the use of lower Q coils. Since we wish to make a crystal set but can't (by definition to keep it a crystal set!) tolerate any powered devices, we'll have to cope with a high-Q resonator at the FM frequency in order to obtain reasonable selectivity. As you'll see, it can be done! Oh yes, there is one more thing: our signals are very feeble. In order to conserve the precious microwatts, we'll need to make sure the resonator is well constructed to produce the Q required and matched to the reset of the set.

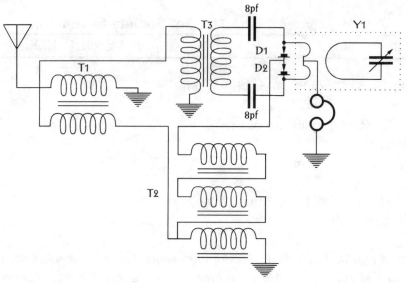

Figure 1: Complete schematic of FM xtal receiver. T1 and T2 are made from TV baluns. T3 is wound from a ferrite bead. D1 and D2 must be chosen carefully.

For simplicity, we'll want to deal with only one high-Q resonator too. Discriminators and ratio detectors used in typical FM sets achieve quadrature and resonance phase-shift by using a double-tuned circuit. These weakly coupled resonators will have a nominal 90 degree phase shift; and with a sufficiently high Q, will exhibit the required phase shift with frequency changes (required for FM detection). However, they work best at a fixed frequency, as both resonators require tuning. This would, obviously, be most inconvenient for crystal receiver purposes, as it would require adjusting two resonators while tuning over the FM band (let alone having to build two!)

Hence, a design requiring only one resonator seems best. In part one, we already outlined how to accomplish this, and Figure 1 shows the complete circuit diagram for just such a receiver. T1 is the 180 degree power splitter, T3 is simply a balun used to generate balanced signals for driving the quadrature network, and T2 is a step-up transformer to raise the impedance of the in-phase signal. Together, Y1 and the 8 pf capacitors form the quadrature network, with the phase detector made from D1 and D2 connected at the high-impedance points. In this configuration, the phase detector is arranged as if it were a single-balanced mixer. Output is taken from the center point at the resonant coupling loops.

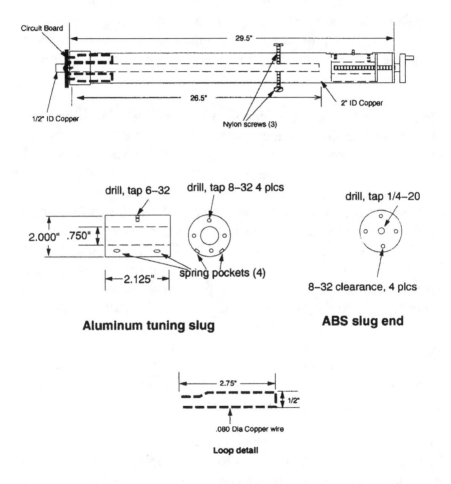

Figure 2: Construction details of tunable coaxial resonator. Small springs, clipped from a ball-point pen, are to ride in the pockets in the tuning slug, to eliminate wobble.

25

The High-Q Resonator

The FM band covers 88 - 108 Mhz with a channel spacing of 200 Khz. Thus, for selectivity, the required loaded Q will be f_0/BW, or about 500. This means that the resonator must have an unloaded Q significantly higher than 500. The easiest way to obtain this at 100 Mhz is with a coaxial resonator. My design requires some metalworking, and I am fortunate to have access to a machine shop. Since this is a prototype design, I carefully machined the tuning mechanism. It is probably more complicated than it needs to be. Perhaps someone can modify my design so that it is easier to build from common hardware.

Figure 2 shows the construction details of the coaxial resonator made from a section of 2 inch copper pipe. The theoretical unloaded Q for these dimensions is about 2000. I measured only 1000. Unfortunately, this had to suffice as the device was already quite large. The center conductor is made from a piece of 1/2 inch copper pipe, soldered into a hole in the center of a 2 inch copper end cap. One very important concern when building the center conductor is that it be as self-supporting as possible. I used three nylon screws near the free end to allow some centering adjustment. Do not use a piece of cardboard, or any other type of rigid support. These will seriously reduce the Q. Make it touch as little "stuff" as possible. Tuning is accomplished by a sliding slug at the free end of the center conductor. Figure 2 shows how a threaded rod can be used to drive it in and out. A small set screw riding in a slot in the 2 inch pipe serves both to prevent its rotation and as a tuning indicator. Some experimentation will be necessary to get the range just right.

There are two coupling loops in this design. Each has a self inductance of about 70nH and is loosely coupled to the resonator. I was able to use a spectrum analyzer and signal generator to measure the performance of my resonator. With one loop as an input, and the other as an output (coupling both through 8 pf caps), I could measure a loaded Q of several hundred, with an insertion loss of 1 dB at the low end and only 3 dB or so at the high end of the band.

Without this equipment, these measurements would be much more difficult. However, it should be possible to rig up an oscillator (say, from an FM wireless mic) and a detector (1N34 and micro-ammeter) to verify the tuning range and loss. In such a endeavor, a nearby FM radio would be very useful as a wavemeter to measure the oscillator frequency.

T3 provides a balanced drive so that the center point of the two loops sees no RF signal. This is a convenient point to take the output, since any stray capacitance at that point will not affect the tuning or matching. The 8 pf capacitors serve to take the 100 ohms of the secondary of T3 and transform it to about 1.6 K ohms. This increases the drive voltage for the diodes, and comes closer to an impedance match for the headphones. Meanwhile, T2 transforms its 100 ohm primary impedance to about 900 ohms to drive the other input of the phase detector. This is not a rigorous match, but is much, much better than doing nothing. Also, it is not clear how to optimize the splitting and matching when a signal must be split along two paths. However, one can argue that roughly equal splitting between the two branches must not be far from the best.

Figure 3 shows the printed circuit board used for this project. This is a double-sided board, with the back side used as a ground plane. It is thus important to clear away some copper around each of the coupling loop mounting holes on the ground side. The large pad in the center can be bored away to fit over the extension of the 1/2 inch pipe. This board is then held to the 2 inch end cap with a single screw, a spacing washer, and a hole tapped in the end cap. Care must be taken to ensure that the coupling loops do not short to the end cap. The clearance holes can be sufficiently oversized.

Transformer Construction Detail

T1 is made from the two-hole core of a common, inexpensive TV balun. After tearing off the case, the transformer can be unsoldered and used unmodified. These coils have extremely low loss in the FM band. T2 is also made from a two-hole balun core, but with new

27

windings. Each winding consists of a full turn (once through each hole). Fine wire, such as number 30 or 34 should be used, and the windings should be tight against the ferrite. T3 is made from a common one-hole ferrite bead. Each winding consists of 2 turns of number 30 wire. Again, windings should be tight. D1 and D2 have many options; see the next section.

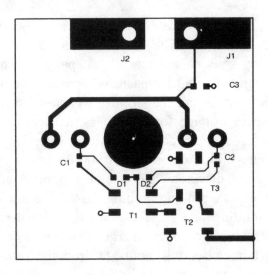

Figure 3: PC board layout for the receiver. J1 and J2 are pads for Fahnestock connectors (which all Xtal sets must use) soldered as surface-mount components. J2 requires a connection to the ground side. Also, several pads are included which must be drilled and connected to ground with short pieces of wire.

Operation

I used a pair of Brandes headphones for this receiver. I also have a pair of Baldwins which work almost as well. Of course, based on cost, it would seem that the reverse should be true. Incidentally, from these measurements, I discovered that my right ear is not nearly as sensitive as my left. This type of knowledge can be useful when tuning crystal receivers.

I began evaluating the performance of the set by using a microvolt generator with an internal FM test tone. I experimented with various germanium diodes, and found a lot of variation. In fact, different diodes claiming to be 1N34s were found to have vastly differing performance. Some 1N34s purchased years ago from Radio Shack were the best. With these, I was able to tune the receiver and detect audio with a sensitivity of - 32dBm. Not being entirely satisfied with these results, I bought some zero-bias Schottky diodes (Metelics MSS20,005-E28) and obtained a sensitivity of -37 dBm. This is pretty good, although it would be interesting to see if one can do better.

Unless you live next door to a radio station, you will need some type of antenna. Radio Shack sells a little FM directional unit for about $20 that works quite well. I ran twin lead line down to a TV balun (those baluns are just so handly!), and connected the unbalanced port to the receiver input. The nearest stations are about 10 miles away, and I could faintly hear two of them. In fact, the two stations I could hear were 105.7 and 106.5. These are easily separated with my high-Q receiver, indicating that its selectivity is quite respectable.

In the process of scanning the horizon and looking for stations, I discovered something very interesting. By turning the antenna for vertical polarization, reception was noticeably better. This requires mounting the antenna on an insulating post (such as a piece of ABS pipe) so as to not affect the vertical signal component. Most FM stations deliver circular polarization, with equal amounts of power in both horizontal and vertical modes. However, at rooftop height, it seems that the vertical component is stronger. One obvious explanation for this is the presence of power lines running horizontally at this level. I suspect that these lines take out the horizontal component quite effectively. In other directions, I was able to detect some other, weaker stations at between 90 and 100 Mhz. By far my best reception is at 105.7, where, ironically, I know the receiver is not nearly as sensitive as at the lower frequencies. Furthermore, there is a large tree in the signal path! VHF propagation is largely by line-of-sight, and is easily affected by obstacles. A single-story rooftop is not the best antenna location. Higher and less obstructed antenna locations will dramatically increase signal strength.

Editor: That's Ed's FM crystal set story. He'd like to hear from anyone who makes a serious attempt to build it - or a variation on this theme for that matter.

TIDBITS

[Editor] In our lead article, Ed mentions using TV baluns. Thinking I might want to try a variation on Ed's set, I made a trip to Radio Shack and purchased two TV- VCR Matching Transformers, Cat. No. 15-1253B. The package says, "For matching 300-ohm antenna leads to 75-ohm F connector." Following Ed's lead, I broke the plastic housing apart - using an exacto-knife, in order to take a look at the two-hole core. Sure enough, there it was, with three loops of two-conductor (silver and copper) speaker wire threaded around each core. At one end of these wires, the two silver leads attached to the two 300-ohm terminals while the two copper leads were tied together and soldered to the ground side of the F connector. At the other end of the loops, the silver and copper wires were split with one soldered to the F connector ground and the other to the F connector center pin. Did you follow that? Did I? That's hard to describe.

MEMBERSHIP CORRESPONDENCE

Dwayne Horton, Wilmore, KY. "Just got vols 4 & 5. Outstanding!...Puett Electronics sells a copy of Bucher's often quoted Wireless Telegraphy. Puett Electronics, PO Box 28572, Dallas, TX 75228. I was wondering - can a choke coil be used as a tuning coil? *[Editor. No, not unless the inductance of the coil is the same as what you might use, or small enough to go with a variable cap, but doubtful. Oh, Dwayne's looking for an original copy of Bucher. Write him at 201 Butler Blvd, Wilmore, KY, 40390.*

Dwayne, check Rainy Day Books PO Box 775, Fitzwilliam, NH 03447 (603) 585-3448.]

Rob, KB8TEJ, Lewisburg, WV. "I am currently working on a 50 Mhz set. I guess if you are into 6-meter AM DX you have an interest in this odd-ball. The coil design is from a 20s 56 Mhz regenerative rig. It detects but local MW broadcasts overwhelm it. Needs a trap. I'll let you know how it goes. *[Editor. Rob, what sort of DX are you finding on 6-meters?]*

Also, Rob sent us an article entitled "How to Become a Wireless Operator VIII - Tuning with a Variable condenser", by T. M. Lewis, Popular Science Monthly. Date published didn't appear at the bottom, just page 629. I'm guessing about 1920? The title implies a bunch of articles. Anybody want to research? Here's a bit from the article on Short Waves.

Tuning to Short Waves. "When it is desired to receive wavelengths which are short compared with the fundamental wavelength of the antenna, it is very convenient to insert a variable condenser in series with the aerial connection, as shown in figure 4."

Eddy Strickland, Warrenton, NC. "Recently purchased a Heathkit CR-1 set in great condition from a friend. He also gave me a Philmore fixed crystal detector, still in the box! The CR-1 works great. If you would like a short article on the CR-1, let me know."

Bill Mitch, N9JTR, Hebron, IN. "I thought you might be interested in the enclosed issue of Nuts & Volts magazine...see the FM crystal set on page 64. I built it but evidently I'm not close enough to a powerful FM station to receive. I could hear a tone using an FM test generator though. I'd like to know if anyone else had any luck with this set?" *[Editor: That was my article Bill! I could receive our 91.5 Mhz station that is seven miles from me...but not strongly. Anyone else?]*

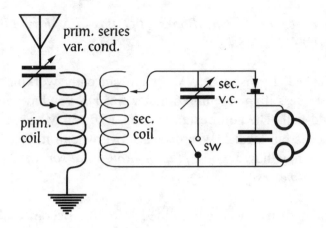

Figure 4: A variable condenser inserted in series with the aerial connection for short wavelengths

In Search for the Perfect Diode?

In our lead article, Ed mentioned using a zero-bias Schottky diode, Metelics MSS20,005-E28. I wonder how close we can come to the perfect diode, no R and zero turn-on voltage? Also, P.A. Kinzie responded to our "tidbit" in the January issue as follows:

"I have not seen an explanation covering the short wave sensitivity of iron pyrites or the other natural minerals, with their witches brew of high content impurities. However, there is an equivalent circuit used to describe the behavior of diode quality germanium and silicon with known dopant amounts. Since the overall behavior of natural and synthetic materials is comparable, perhaps a similar equivalent circuit can be applied to natural crystals.

The equivalent circuit shown in the sketch below can be used with doped germanium and silicon. Here R is the non-linear resistance responsible for rectifying action, C is an equivalent capacitance which bypasses some of the current which would otherwise flow through R, and r is a fixed resistance dependent upon material bulk properties and point contact geometry. Both R and C occur in a thin barrier layer at and near the semiconductor surface. C is said to range from 0.2 to 2.0 pf for standard materials available at the time of publication.

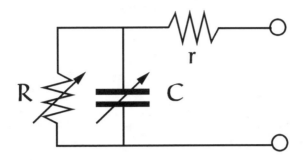

Figure 5: Natural diode equivalent circuit.

If this model can be applied to iron pyrites and other such crystals, it is evident that if C were small for iron pyrites as compared with, say galena, iron pyrites would perform better in the short wave region. I hope that some of the readers will come up with a more specific explanation."

CRYSTAL SET CONTEST!

The Society will be publishing a Crystal Set projects book this fall. Plans are to cover projects that beginners can follow and that people can build with their children. We are also hoping to distribute this projects book to schools and clubs. If you would like to submit a project to be considered for the book the deadline is August 30th. We will seriously consider any project that is easy to follow and well tested. If your project is chosen for the book you will receive $50 and 5 copies of the book. Projects can be handwritten and figures hand drawn, there are no rules! Any questions call Rebecca in the office at (314)725-1172.

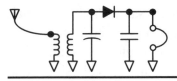

The Xtal Set Society Newsletter

Volume 6, No. 3   May 1, 1996

A CRYSTAL HEADPHONE FROM A CAT FOOD CAN
by William E. Simes

It seems an accepted tenet among crystal set builders that the headphone is too sophisticated to fabricate at home and must therefore be produced commercially. Therein lies a challenge.

Once there were commercial high impedance headphones that exploited the remarkable piezoelectric properties of Rochelle Salt. Piezoelectric phenomenon that, you may recall, occurs when a crystal subjected to mechanical strain generates an electric field within itself. The converse piezoelectric effect occurs when an electric field causes a change in the shape of the crystal. It is this latter effect that drives crystal headphones and other transducers. Of the naturally occurring piezoelectric crystals, Rochelle Salt is by far the most active. Even so, crystal dimensional changes caused by the voltage levels normally fed to a headphone would be minuscule. So, how then do crystal headphones work?

The question is answered in C. W. Sawyer's 1931 paper, "The Use of Rochelle Salt Crystals for Electrical Reproducers and Microphones."[1] Sawyer's transducer used two adjacent crystal bars with electrodes configured such that an applied voltage caused one bar to expand and the other to contract thus causing the assembly to bend. He likened this to the action of the familiar bimetallic thermostat, an arrangement which greatly magnifies minute dimensional changes. Later writings refer to Sawyer's twin crystal arrangement as "bimorphs." A further revelation found in Sawyer's paper was the behavior of Rochelle Salt in an electric field. The edges of a rectangular plane Rochelle salt crystal slab, cut perpendicular to its electric axis, can be viewed as a parallelogram. The parallelogram is undergoing shear strain in an electric field such that the vertical axes of the slab lean with a direction and magnitude dependent on the amplitude and polarity of the applied field.

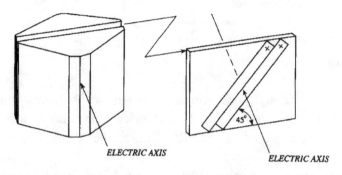

1. Cut crystal slab perpendicular to electric axis.

2. Cut bars from crystal slab so that their length is 45 deg. from the horizontal axis. Mark crystal face " + " on bars before cutting.

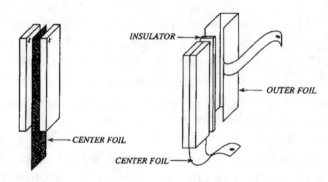

3. Super glue bars to center foil with marked faces positioned as shown.

4. Glue insulator to assembled bars then glue on outside foil to complet the bimorph.

Figure 1: Bimorph "Rochelle Salt" Assembly

To apply the information from Sawyer's paper empirically, one must first have a suitable Rochelle Salt crystal. There are several texts on growing crystals at home such as "Crystals and Crystal Growing," by Alan Holden and Phylis Morrison[2]. The book is still in print and should be available from your local library. It includes a number of crystal growing recipes including one for Rochelle crystal. Follow the instructions carefully, and with patience you can grow a flawless crystal.

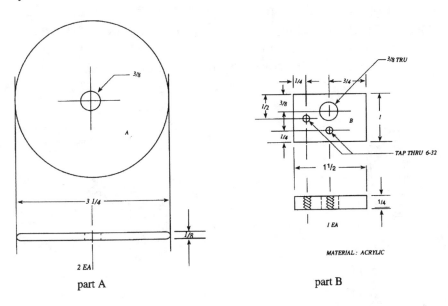

part A   part B

Figure 2: Acrylic Mounting Parts

Harvest your crystal(s) when the distance between the two flat surfaces is about two centimeters. If you can find Rochelle Salt commercially from which to mix your growing solution, that would be the easiest. Or you can make your own as I did. While the crystal grows you will have ample time to build a jig for cutting the crystal. I cut my crystals with a band saw using a jig I designed. Once a crystal is harvested and the cutting jig is completed, cut a slab from the crystal as shown in step 1 of Figure 1. This step is somewhat paradoxical in that a thick slab is needed for structural strength while working with the fragile crystal. On the other hand, a thin slab is needed to assure greater bending flexibility and a higher electric field, both of which would enhance sensitivity. I have succeeded in cutting and working with slabs as thin as 3/32 inch. Slab surfaces can be made smoother (and thinner) with careful hand sanding using 150 grit paper taped to a flat surface. When a slab of desired thickness is ready, proceed with the remaining steps of Figure 1. Make sure the crystal orientation is marked on the slab before bars are cut. I've had good luck with bars 1/4 to 3/8 inches wide and 1-1/4 inches long. The bar length is, of course, limited by the width of the slab. Bimorphs built following the steps in Figure 1 have worked well in the simple headphone described next.

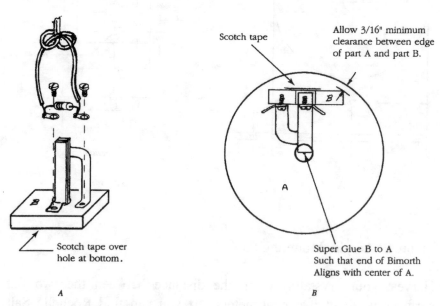

Figure 3: Bimorph Subassembly

The instructions that follow are intended to demonstrate just how simple building a functional high-impedance crystal headphone can be, but first a little background and description. For starters, let's assume that few of us put empty cat food cans over our ears and listen intently. If, however, you were to perform this experiment you could hear nearly anything that brushed against the bottom of the can, even items as subtle as a piece of thread. This suggests the can bottom might make an effective diaphragm for a sound transducer. So, in the model that follows, the can bottom (diaphragm), together with the can sides, provide an effective housing for a drive mechanism. The drive mechanism is then mounted to a plastic disk at the open end of the can. A similar disk bonded to the peripheral ridge on the closed end of our can protects this "diaphragm" and serves as an ear pad.

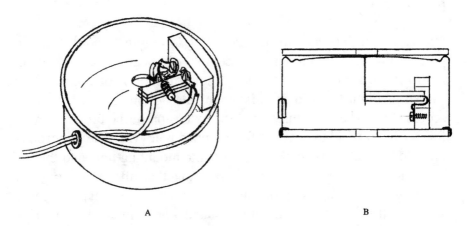

A   B

Figure 4: Final Assembly

Materials to build the device are as follows:

1   bimorph assembled per Figure 1
1   1 inch straight pin
1   5.5 oz cat food can with pull tab opener
        either: Alpo steel can (.007 in. thick)
        or Friskies aluminum (.009 in. thick)
1   100K 1/8w resistor (Radio Shack)
1   1/4 inch grommet (Radio Shack)
2   6-32x1/4 inch machine screws
2   #6 lugs
4ft #24 AWG stranded 2 conductor speaker wire (Radio Shack)

As-required materials:

Reynolds Wrap aluminum (.0015 inch)
Super Glue
Devcon 5-minute Epoxy
Scotch tape
1/8 inch acrylic (for part A Fig. 2)
1/4 inch acrylic (for part B Fig. 2)
rosin core solder

Once a bimorph is constructed according to Figure 1 and the acrylic parts of Figure 2 are fabricated, assembly can begin. Step one, then, is to mount a bimorph in the large hole of part B (of Figure 2) as shown in Figure 3. To do this, cover the bottom of the hole with scotch tape. Then carefully bend the extension of the bimorph inner foil so that it will lap over the front tapped hole when the bimorph is mounted. Make sure the bimorph fits the mounting hole and that its inner and outer foils won't be shorted together after mounting. If shorting appears to be a problem, use a small piece of tape or paper to assure the foils are electrically isolated when mounted. Now mix a small amount of epoxy and mount the bimorph as shown in Figure 3. Avoid epoxy on the foil areas which will later be used for making electrical contact. While the epoxy cures, separate the wires at one end of the lead cable for three inches or so and tie a fire underwriter's knot. This will keep the lead from slipping through the grommet after final assembly. Strip and tin the wire ends. Solder one lead and one end of the 100K resistor to a #6 lug. Solder the remaining lead and the other resistor lead to another #6 lug. When the epoxy sets, use a sharp pencil to punch through the bimorph lead foils where they cross the tapped holes. Mount the lugs at these locations with 6-32 x 1/4 inch screws. Trim excess foil from the mountings with a razor blade or an Exacto knife. A thin coating of Super Glue on exposed surfaces of the crystal will protect it from moisture. When the glue cures, this assembly is ready to mount to a disk (part A of Figure 2). Super Glue part B to part A, as shown in Figure 3B, so that the free end of the bimorph aligns with the center of the hole in part A and all parts of the assembly clear the edge of the disk by at least 3/16 inch. If the bimorph is too long to meet both requirements, then let its end extend beyond the hole center. The 3/16 inch edge clearance must be maintained for the assembly to fit the can.

Final Assembly

Punch a quarter-inch diameter hole in the side of the can with a hand-held paper punch. The hole location isn't critical. Now insert the grommet.   Mark the center of the can bottom with a black marker pen. Then, make several measurements to the center of the bottom and scribe these locations in the blackened area. A centering head on a combination square works well for this. Once the center is located, punch a pin hole there without deforming the bottom. This can be done by placing the can over a large wood dowel secured vertically in a vise, then driving a needle through the center into the dowel. The black marking can then be removed from the can with Gumout or some other suitable solvent. Insert the working assembly lead wire through the grommet from inside the can. Check to see that the working assembly seats properly on the ledge at the open end of the can. When satisfied with the seating, remove the assembly and coat the ledge with super glue.   Then mount the working assembly as shown in Figure 4A. Set a weight on the assembly and let the glue harden. Insert a straight pin through the bottom hole as shown in Figure 4B. Temporarily secure the pin head to the can with a piece of scotch tape. Invert the can and working through the hole in part A, fasten the pin to the end of the bimorph with super glue. A toothpick is an effective tool for this operation. When the glue hardens, remove the tape holding the pin head and secure the head to the can with super glue. When the glue securing the pin head hardens, mount the remaining part A disk over the bottom of the can with several strips of scotch tape. This last disk becomes the ear pad as well as the "diaphragm" protector. That operation completes the headphone assembly. If desired, a phone plug or other connector may be added to the free end of the lead wire.

A note explaining the resistor across the bimorph may be in order. Recall that in a crystal set, the diode detector applies to the earphone half sinusoidal voltages at radio frequency, the amplitude of which is defined by the audio modulation. It follows then, that the diode output is of only one polarity. The unloaded bimorph acts as a capacitor which tends to charge to the peak voltage. Without an adequate discharge path, the voltage can't faithfully follow the modulating signal; hence distortion. The shunting resistor provides the needed discharge path to essentially eliminate this mode of distortion.

References

[1] C. Baldwin Sawyer, Proceedings of the Institute of Radio Engineers, Vol. 10. No. 11, November 1931, pp 2020-2029.

[2] Alan Holden and Phylis Morrison, Crystals and Crystal Growing, 10th printing (The MIT Press, Cambridge, MA 1995)

[Editor: A special thanks to Bill's nephew Tim Barnhart for completing the figures on his computer. Thanks for your help!]

MEMBERSHIP CORRESPONDENCE

Paul Dennis, Tucson, AZ. "Your contest for simple projects is great. I have been volunteering at the middle school and have had such a thing in mind. We have built small solar powered cars and simple electric motors. I think Xtal sets could be next!"

Robert Ellis, Derby, England. "An article in The Daily Telegraph about the society took me back over twenty years. The interest in crystal technology started in childhood and was resurrected last year when a Long-Wave powerhouse AM rocker opened over the Irish Sea. I made my nephew a straight single-channel set for 252Khz with voltage-doubler detection and it works so well, the bug has bit again!"

Jim Hill, Palos Verdes Estates, CA. "I will be retiring in May of 1996 and intend to get back to building crystal sets and regenerative receivers for DXing. I would like to correspond with others with similar interests, 3801 Palos Verdes Drive North, Palos Verdes Estates, CA 90274-1159 ph 310-378-4411."

Bill Gerrey, San Francisco, CA. "In the correspondence section of the July 95 issue, I tripped over the letter from Ron Pearce, alluding to his acorn 955 set. I want this badly, as I have a small supply of 955's in the junk box. It would make me fairly squeak to have the schematic diagram and coil data. Help! Also, since receivers, at least for some time, were licensed in England, I wonder if home-brew sets were a way to squeeze past the license fee? 154 Hermann St., San Francisco, CA 94102.

WANTED: CRYSTAL SET PROJECTS

We have received some great responses, but we need more! The Society will be publishing a Crystal Set Projects book this fall. Our plans are to cover projects that beginners can follow and that people can build with their children. We are also hoping to distribute this projects book to schools and clubs. If you would like to submit a project to be considered for the book the deadline is August 30th. We will seriously consider any project that is easy to follow and well tested. If your project is chosen for the book you will receive $50 and 5 copies of the book. Projects can be handwritten and figures hand drawn, there are no rules! Any questions call Rebecca in the office at (314)725-1172.

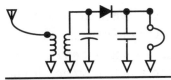

The Xtal Set Society Newsletter

Volume 6, No. 4   July 1, 1996

THE DEN TWO CRYSTAL RADIO
by Alan R. Klase

[Editor: Alan sent this design in to our Crystal Set Projects Contest, and we've decided that he is already a winner! Many members have called wanting to know what kind of projects we are looking for, so we decided to print his as an example. This project along with step-by-step instructions will appear in our projects book scheduled for publication this fall.]

I noted your call for crystal set projects in the May edition. It just so happens that I have a project left over from my term as Cub Scout Den Leader. By the way, this is a better than average crystal set.

I wanted my guys to enjoy the experience of hearing a radio they had built with their own hands out of common materials. Radio projects have been a part of scouting for a long, long, time.

I had several goals in mind when I did this design. First I wanted the boys to do as much of the assembly as possible, including their own coil. Secondly, the design needed to be reproducible by others, and not require hard to get or expensive components. Finally, the set needed to be a reasonably good performer. We were located in the deep suburbs of Philadelphia, with no strong local stations, so a really simple design would only work with a long antenna. Most parents would want to throw a little wire into a tree or stretch it out in the attic, and have the set play.

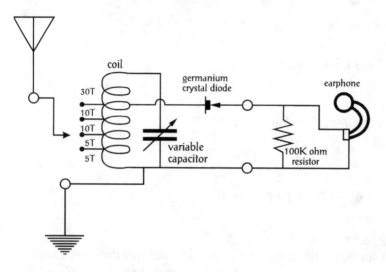

Figure 1: Schematic Diagram

The design that emerged, The Den Two Crystal Radio, is described as follows. The set is a single tuned parallel circuit comprising a tapped spider-web coil and a variable capacitor of approximately 365pF maximum capacity. The base of the set is a piece of pine shelving board, and the front panel is 1/4" plywood. The detector, a Radio Shack germanium diode, is connected to the center tap of the 60 turn coil. The coil has three additional taps to accommodate a variety of antennas. Crystal earphones from Mouser Electronics were employed because of their availability and high performance to cost ratio. A 100K ohm resistor in parallel with the headset provides a DC load for the detector circuit, and avoids the distortion reported by other experimenters.

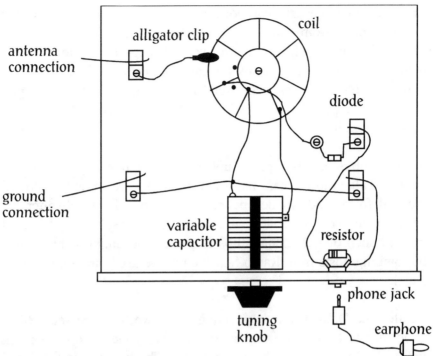

Figure 2: Pictorial Diagram

The spiderweb coil was chosen because it is easy for young people to wind. Nine-year olds have neither the manual dexterity nor attention span to do a good job of winding a cylindrical coil. The forms were cut from 1/8" Plexiglas using a scroll saw. Similar plastic material is sold in home centers to replace the glass in storm doors. Number 26 enameled "magnet wire" was used. Anything between #24 and #28 should be acceptable. About 60 feet of wire is required. The taps are created by twisting a small eyelet at the appropriate places as the coil is being wound. A crochet hook is a good tool for doing this. You'll need to scrape the insulation off the taps and the two ends of the wire. It's a good idea to spread the taps out to avoid short circuits. Make the first tap at 5 turns and the second at 10 1/9 turns, and so on. Be careful that all turns are wound in the same direction. It's easy to get confused when creating a tap, and then start winding in the opposite direction.

The crucial parts are the earphone and the variable capacitor. Order the earphones from Mouser Electronics. This is the only easily accessible source. The best bet for variable capacitors is to scrounge them wherever you can. Look for knobs at the same time! You can purchase 365pF variable capacitors from Antique Electronic Supply also, but it is perfectly acceptable to use a two section cap out of a junk clock radio.

For the Cub Scouts I spent a couple of months rounding up caps and knobs. Talked to the ham radio old timers! I precut and predrilled the coil forms and wooden parts. It's a good idea to chamfer the edges of the coil form slots to avoid scraped insulation. I lucked into a bunch of Fahnestock clips for input and output connections, but binding posts from Radio Shack could be used through the front panel.

I called the Dads in for the meeting when we built the sets. It's a good idea to have a working sample for everyone to copy. I stuck with solder for some of the connections. The kids can at least feed the solder into the joints.

All told, we build eight of these sets. Almost all of them were later set up at home, and everyone was suitably impressed. I was pleased to have had the opportunity to expose young people to radio in this elementary and hands-on way.

SOUNDS VINTAGE

Ron Pearce, one of our members from England, recently wrote in suggesting we add a new section to the newsletter with logs of stations heard and a description of the receiver used. Great idea Ron! Ron was recently interviewed by one of England's national papers, "The Daily Telegraph" concerning his interest in crystal radio, and the Xtal Set Society was listed. Welcome to all our new members in the U.K.!

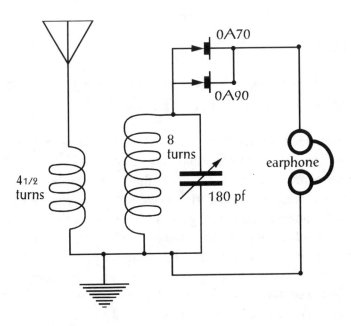

Figure 3: Ron Pierce Crystal Set

Here is how Ron described his set, "The coil covers 19-41M shortwave. The antenna is a loft mounted inverted V. After many hours of experimenting I found the enclosed circuit to be the most sensitive and selective so far (see Figure 3). The coil is a ½" dia x 2½" plastic tube with plastic coated stiff bell wire."

Station	Date	Time
Vatican Radio	2-22-96	20.25
Radio Spain	2-23-96	16.38
Radio France Int	2-25-96	21.18
Radio Canada Int	2-26-96	14.55
Radio Sweden	2-28-96	18.53
Radio Israel	2-28-96	20.03
V.O.A.	3-4-96	19.31
Radio Budapest	3-4-96	20.17
Radio Denmark	3-12-96	11.56
All India Radio	3-20-96	11.50
Radio Kuwait	3-21-96	18.14

TIDBITS

[Editor: Here's a bit from "How to Become a Wireless Operator, Part VIII, Popular Science Monthly, by Tim Lewis, ~1930]

"There has been some dispute as to whether a secondary tuning condenser, connected in the usual way, shown in [Figure 4], aids in producing a receiver more effective than the simple "broad tuned secondary" circuit. Extended trials have shown beyond a doubt that the sharply tuned circuit of Figure 4, when properly adjusted, will give greater selectivity for the same strength signals than the circuit without variable condenser in the secondary. By building the secondaries specially to suit each case, about the same maximum signals are secured with looser coupling between primary and secondary. As a result, the tuning is sharper and interference is much reduced. The practical actions of such tuners should be studied in detail by every operator, and the differences in operation dependent upon closing and opening the condenser 'switch' in the secondary ciruit should be particulary noted."

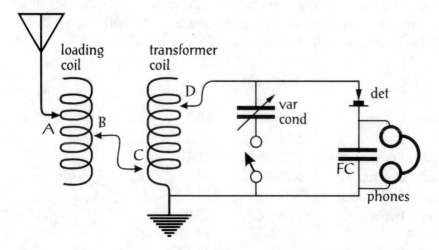

Figure 4: The receiver is set up by combining the tuning coils with the variable condenser

MEMBERSHIP CORRESPONDENCE

Clarence Janos, W8TNI, Cleveland, OH. Clarence wrote, "I have the Crystal Set Handbook Vol III and enjoy reading it. I have a lot of magazines, mostly from the 1940s. I Found an article titled 'Germanium Diode Broadcast-Band Tuner' in the May 1956 issue of Radio & Television News that I thought readers might enjoy." [Editor. Clarence is referring to, of course, the Miller Company's famous tuner. Evidently 1956 was the year they introduced it since the article mentions a "tuner recently introduced in kit form by J.W. Miller Company."]

Harold Wilkey, Mount Vernon, ME. "There's a neat article - a contest entry - using the coherer in the June 1993 issue of RF Design; see page 84." [Editor. Jim Escoffier's entry describes an AM radio using early-1900s technology for the front-end and detector and an MC1454G IC for audio boost. As you may recall, coherers conduct when RF is applied, and Jim has used the speaker coil to restore it for the next RF surge. Cute!] Jim states, "By using mechanical feedback for decohering, some resemblance to the original modulation might be maintained, but the resulting audio would probably not be high fidelity." Jim goes on to say, "...coherer can be replaced with a crystal. The crystal can be made by sprinkling a little powdered sulphur over a spot of melted solder. A few seconds of feeling around on the residue of the sulphur with a cat whisker will produce a couple of sensitive spots." Anybody tried a detector like this?

Gary Friedlander, WD9HDM, Buffalo Grove, IL. "First of all, I'd like to say I really enjoy the Xtal newsletter. Although I enjoy all sorts of high tech gadgets (internet and PCs), there is nothing better than hearing a station come through on a crystal set built from scratch! In particular, I like to experiment with 'Slinkys' as antennas."

"In many catalogs, I've seen a product called the Omnipotent AM Antenna. Is there a home brew device which is just as effective?" [Editor. Anyone know about this potent antenna?]

Roy Osborne, Council Bluffs, IA. "Been working on several ideas to build and report on such as a loop antenna amplifier for crystal set front-end, infinite impedance detector for real loose coupling & hi Q, traps and boosters, and possibly regenerative stuff. Enjoy reading - and rereading! - the newsletter; some of it takes some head scratching!" [Editor. Thanks Roy. Sounds like fun stuff!]

Robert G. Everding, Ballwin, MO. "I have been building crystal sets for over 50 years and have had great success lately using a crystal earphone with a high impedance of 100,000 ohms. I have purchased this earphone for many years from Etco Electronics...but have been informed that they are no longer in business. I would appreciate any information you can provide me as to where I can obtain crystal earphones." [Editor: You're not alone Robert; we've had many folks writing in asking about parts! Please look at this issue's vendor section.]

Art Redman, Portland, OR. "I became interested in the Society after reading the article "A Ground-Noise Powered Receiver" in your newsletter of September 1, 1995 by Bill Simes. Enclosed find copies of two articles which may be of interest to other xtal set builders. From Popular Electronics magazine of October, 1958 p. 49-50 is the article "Stolen Power Transistor Radio." Also is a copy of U.S. patent no. 2,818,242 dated November 12, 1957 invented by Lloyd R. Crump titled, "Powering Electrical Devices with Energy Abstracted from the Atmosphere" showing a transistor radio receiver. The copy comes from The Free Energy Device Handbook by David Hatcher Childress: Adventures Unlimited Press, Stelle, Illinois, 1994, p. 254.

FOX HOLE RADIO REVISITED

Jamie Jensen, Arden Hills, MN. "Your information was correct...I went to the U of M library and found the October 1962 Popular Mechanics article. Our construction differed from the article in that we used 26 gauge magnet wire but wrapped it on a toilet paper roll instead of a piece of wood. We were unable to find a 'quenched blue' razor blade so we settled for a regular double sided blade. We were also unable to find high impedance earphones so used an old earpiece out of a very old telephone. We used a pencil detector; however, after the lead fell out we found the wire holding the pencil worked too! The radio worked! [Editor. Old telephone earphones? Hm! Has anyone else tried this. We ought to follow up on that! It appears Jamie and his son had a really good time! Pure crystal radio fun! Thanks for reporting Jamie!]

UNCLE PHIL'S CRYSTAL MIND BENDERS!
by Phil Anderson

From time to time we've had a section in the newsletter titled "Tidbits." These little morsels are usually facts or rules of thumb about a component or circuit. The ideas presented are not earth shaking to say the least! Perhaps we should have another section titled Mind Benders, a collection of far out or weird ideas who's origin might be considered the crystal set—after all, doesn't everything come from the crystal set! Oh well, here's my first Mind Bender.

What could you think of that is a mechanical analog to the crystal set? The cool thing about a crystal set is that it doesn't require any external power; the set uses the power of the received signal to operate—to provide you with pure spring water audio! So I'll state it again, is there a mechanical equivalent to the electronic crystal set? Turn that one over in your mind. You might be surprised what you come up with.

Here's one example of many: the old fashioned mill. The river delivers its "signal" and the mill grinds the grain, using the power of the river! How about this one: we eat the cow and then we are able to think! Strange? The food is our "signal" and we operate on the power it delivers to us. Perhaps that one is too weird. An aside, would that make us AM or FM? I guess that would be bio-crystal, not mechno-crystal. Here's another bio then: The tomato plant takes its "signal" from the earth and the sun, producing food for us in a different form. In all these cases—and including the crystal set too—energy is delivered from one thing to another. Crystal sets absorb energy from electromagnetic waves; the mill obtains energy from the flowing river; the plant obtains energy from earth and sky.

The real twist on all this is that nearly everything around us that is not man made is a crystal set analog. It's just that when we came along and built "external" power supplies and engines and such that the "original" or pure power sourcessuch as the radio signal itself—were not longer needed, at least not—directly, to provide us with what we wanted! Hm........we don't eat grains much anymore—the original "signal" food; we eat processed foods like burgers, a twinky or two, hot dogs, etc—that's "external power supply" food! Our hat is off to those folks eating organic foods. Perhaps they listen at night to retransmitted programs of The Shadow on a crystal set too? You think?

I'll leave you with this one, and it might not be crystal set based! If you decided to measure the shoreline of a local lake, would you get the same answer if you used a yardstick and then a 12 inch ruler? How much longer might the shoreline be when you measure it with the foot ruler? It's true you know! Rule: you must measure the shoreline right at the water edge. Uncle Phil.

VENDORS

Bradford Whitecotton, Bossier City, LA. "Where can I find crystal parts today?" Brad, you can buy crystal earphones from us or Mouser, and a number of crystal radio parts from MIDCO. There are others too. It's been a bit since we've listed these regular suppliers so here are a few good ones:

Mouser Electronics, 800-346-6873, TX and CA locations.

MIDCO, P.O. Box 2288 Hollywood, FL, 33020 (954) 925-3670.

The Xtal Set Society, 365pf variable caps, crystal earplugs, working on more! 1-800-927-1771.

WANTED: CRYSTAL SET PROJECTS

We have received some great responses, but we need more! The Society will be publishing a Crystal Set Projects book this fall. Our plans are to cover projects that beginners can follow and that people can build with their children. We are also hoping to distribute this projects book to schools and clubs. If you would like to submit a project to be considered for the book the deadline is August 30th. We will seriously consider any project that is easy to follow and well tested. If your project is chosen for the book you will receive $50 and 5 copies of the book. Projects can be handwritten and figures hand drawn, there are no rules! Any questions call Rebecca in the office at (314)725-1172.

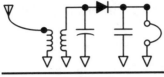

The Xtal Set Society Newsletter

Volume 6, No. 5   September 1, 1996

FROM CRYSTAL SET TO SUPERHETE: THE SEARCH FOR SENSITIVITY AND SELECTIVITY by Phil Anderson, WØXI

Ever since Marconi demonstrated "wireless" in 1895, radio engineers have strived to improve receiver performance, both sensitivity and selectivity. Sensitivity is defined as a measure of how well a receiver can pick up weak signals, and selectivity is a measure of how well a receiver separates signals received.

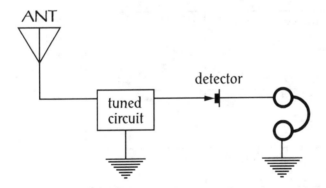

Figure 1: Crystal Set.

Modern day FM receivers have a sensitivity of 0.5 uV (microvolts) or better, and to the surprise of many, a well designed crystal set is equally sensitive. This is due to the fact that the human ear is more sensitive than any radio receiver. Selectivity, however, has been the real challenge for designers — and continues to be. Crystal sets can compete with today's commercial radio receivers on selectivity but if and only if sensitivity is sacrificed.

It's interesting to trace the evolution of radio receiver design to see how our fellow radio experimenters and engineers managed (finally!) to overcome the initial inability to achieve selectivity while maintaining sensitivity. It took them over thirty years, from Marconi's initial demonstration to the invention of the superhete, to achieve selectivity and sensitivity in the same set. Let's examine the evolution of sets along this radio-brick-road; it's an interesting journey. See Table 1 for a quick summary and Figures 1 through 5 for the block diagrams of these sets.

Table 1

SETS	TIMELINE
crystal	around 1900
tuned radio frequency (TRF)	1920s
regenerative & super regenerative (regens)	1920s
reflex	1920s
superheterodyne (superhetes)	late 1920s
frequency modulation	1930s
digital	1990s

THE CRYSTAL SET. While taking many forms, this basic set always consists of a tuned circuit(s), an antenna, a detector of some sort, and headphones. No battery power is added to the set. Good sensitivity is achieved at the expense of selectivity, and long distance HF as well as broadcast band (BC) reception is possible.

The set is capable of amplitude (AM) and frequency modulation reception (FM). The most outstanding features of the crystal set are no requirement for external power and "crystal clear" audio.

TUNED RADIO FREQUENCY SET. Once tubes appeared, radio frequency amplifier stages were added to the front of the crystal set. These stages helped boost the radio frequency signal, thus improving sensitivity, and selectivity improved somewhat.

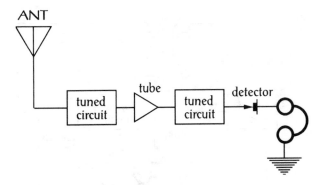

Figure 2: Tuned Radio Frequency Set.

REGENERATIVE AND SUPERREGENERATIVE SETS. Again, with tubes—or "valves" if you prefer, regeneration was possible and was used to boost the strength of the signal. Excellent sensitivity could be achieved, yet tuning was often difficult. Regeneration is the process of feeding a signal back onto itself in proper phase in order to build up it's strength.

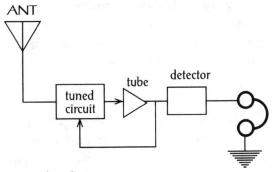

Figure 3: Regenerative Set.

REFLEX SET. Since tubes were very expensive in the 1920s—as a percentage of weekly salary—the reflex circuit was born. It was a "cute" invention; engineers used the same tube for both radio frequency and audio frequency amplification. The signal was boosted by the tube (in a TRF configuration), detected, and then the audio was "run through" the tube again for more amplification. Capacitors and radio frequency chokes were used to separate the radio and audio frequency signals where necessary.

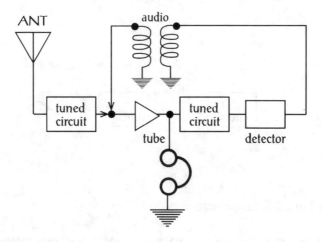

Figure 4: Reflex Set.

THE SUPERHETERODYNE. This set finally achieved what the others could not, selectivity with sensitivity—and all across the broadcast band at that! Selectivity is achieved by converting the radio frequency (RF) signal to a much lower intermediate frequency (IF) so that selectivity and signal amplification can be achieved easily and simultaneously. I suppose that the following finally occurred to someone.... *Since I can achieve/design a circuit at 455 kilohertz (kHz) that is both sensitive and selective, all I have to do to achieve selectivity is to convert the radio frequency signal first to that lower frequency.* Hence the process of heterodyning (multiplication —beating of two signals together) was applied to radio receivers. Piano players and musicians were already familiar with this phenomenon for a century or two. Play two notes at the same time and your ear will hear two others, the sum of the original two notes and the difference, called beat notes.

For those of you who love algebra, it's easy to see that multiplying two sinewaves (radio frequency signals) together produces two other radio signals. You can use the difference signal, (a-b), as your IF signal.

Asin(a) * Bsin(b) =
0.5*AB*cos(a-b) - 0.5*AB* cos(a+b)

Multiplication can be accomplished with a single tube or transistor circuit. Modern integrated circuit (IC) radio chips use a differential pair amplifier.

FREQUENCY MODULATION SET. To the surprise of many, an FM set is exactly an AM set except for the detector. Modern FM sets use a quadrature detector (see our FM crystal set article a few issues back) for FM detection; early sets used a double-tuned circuit, two detectors and a special transformer.

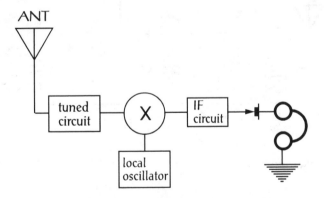

Figure 5: The Superheterodyne Set.

THE DIGITAL SET. Today, radio reception can be accomplished using digital means; that is, we can use a microcomputer to detect radio signals. Most sets using this technique convert the RF signal to an IF signal and then have the computer "digitally" convert the IF to audio. Theoretically, assuming the computer is fast enough, the whole process can be done by computer. That will eventually be a reality.

Finally, to demonstrate that no idea is ever really new, the pioneers of radio had a digital radio working but perhaps did not look at it that way. Just fifty years later we're at it again, but using microcomputers instead of a motor and cam shaft! See Figure 6, the early day digital radio, or "Tikker."

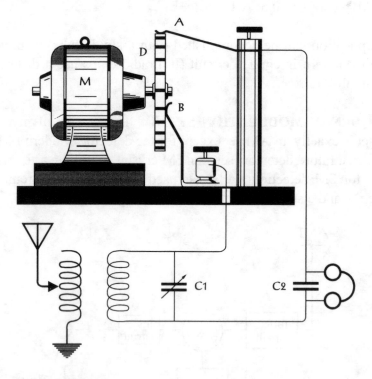

Figure 6: The Tikker

References:

Kinzie, P.A., Crystal Radio: History, Fundamentals, and Design, The Xtal Set Society, St. Louis, MO, 1996.

Anderson, Phil, "The Tikker Detector Revisited," The Crystal Set Handbook, The Xtal Set Society, St. Louis, MO, 1994, page 44.

Demaw, Doug, "Build a Simple Regenerative Receiver for the BC Band," Monitoring Times, January, 1992.

MEMBERSHIP CORRESPONDENCE

Jim Shattuck, Papillion, NE wrote us on the internet asking, "I have seen many references to German-Silver wire for use as a catwhisker. Any idea what it is and where it can be obtained?" [Editor: We don't know, Jim. Can anyone else help with this question?]

Chris Peters, Suffolk, VA. "I am interested in receiving a copy of the newsletter.... At one time in my youth (many moons ago) I built crystal sets to amuse myself and would now like to rekindle the joy of spending the night reposed upon the bathroom floor, ground wire clamped to the sweaty copper pipe and fingers numb from tuning the coils, and share it with my sons." [Editor: We did that also many moons ago!]

Authur Mechler, Cincinnati, OH. "I am a old radio man from the 30's...and inquiring about a RADAK-13, a one tube set of good design. I have all the parts for this, but the panel has been busted, does anyone have any information on this set?"

David Krucas, San Diego, CA has been corresponding with us over the internet. "I built the receiver described in The Design of Unpowered Receivers in the first three issues of the '95 xtal society newsletter. It was wound with homemade litz wire on a 5 inch coil form and used a 3 part variable capacitor. I took a multi-section open frame variable capacitor and measured each section with a capacitance tester at work. Then I used a motor tool and a microscope and removed the small piece of the rotor that sticks through the insulating fiber which connects the rotor plates. I removed a plate at a time with needle nose pliers and tested the capacitance of each section. I was able to reduce the maximum capacitance of each section one plate at a time until I matched the specifications in the article. Then I made the litż wire by taping strands of 39 gauge wire along the wall, and after twisting it by hand, I walked down the hall slowly winding the wire on the 5 inch cardboard tube. Then I strung about 220 feet of wire in my attic, up one side to the top and down the other, crossing over and going back up and down again many times. The radio is the most selective receiver I have ever made. I really enjoy listening to it. I never realized a crystal radio could play so loud. "

David also wrote us about crystal earphones, "My dad, born 1927, told me that they used to test headphones by touching one of the phone tips on their tongue and tapping the other on a tooth filling while wearing the phones. Very faint clicks or a scratching sound can be heard, as well as irritating the heck out of the tooth. I have found that this also works with crystal earphones. Thank you for a great and interesting newsletter."

Scott Thomas, Lexington, KY. "Last week I spent a day at the Wright Patterson Air Force Base Museum. While walking by displays of things made by POWs during WW-II, I noticed a few radios and a crystal radio that appeared to have been made from a broken aircraft radio. The crystal is just barely visible and appears to be sitting in a bottlecap...anyway, thought some members might like to see the exhibit if in KY! In response to Gary Fredlander's questions about the omnipotent AM antenna...yes, it's a very simple device. Just a tank circuit with a large coil. Some years ago I wound a coil around a cigar box, connected it to an antenna and ground, and placed it near my clock radio. The stations came rolling in! It's almost too easy to build.

Jim Nix, Foley, MN. [Editor: Jim sent a listing of radio broadcasting stations from a book published by the Catholic Order of Foresters, 1928-29.] "Many of these stations are still in existence but on different frequencies and with more power. CFCA, CHIC, CHNC, CJSC, etc. [Editor: I note that most, in 1928-29, had fairly low power. Most of the more than one-hundred listed had an output power of just 500 watts. I had the impression early on in this hobby that the early stations were all clear channel, i.e. 50,000 watts. Not so!]

John Eaheart, Plano, TX. "I'm including a drawing of a crystal set that was made for my son while he was in the Cub Scouts about 30 years ago. It was fabricated by empirical guess, but it works."

"At present, my antenna is about 30 feet long and it works, but not as good as when I had a much longer wire. Tune capacitor for station and adjust slider for maximum volume."

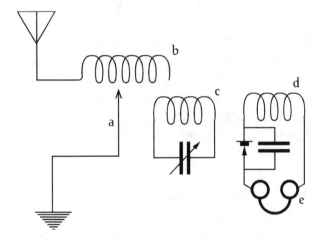

Figure 7: John's Crystal Set

a   slider

b   about 2½" diameter by 6" long

c   wound to resonate over AM band
         on 1½" form

d   free wound on form to fit inside resonate circuit, with about
         fifty turns

e   2K ohm or better

Charles R. Glover, Camarillo, CA. Charles sent us a bit of information on the Heathkit Crystal Receiver Model CR-1. I don't know if they still offer it. The set is pretty flexible, judging from the schematic. There is an antenna coil in series with a 365 pf tuning cap, and the coil is also inductively coupled to another 365 tuning cap to form the tank circuit. The detector diode is tapped down half-way on the secondary of that coupling transformer, and the anode of the diode attaches to one side of the headphones. Additional capacitance can be switched across the antenna tuning capacitor, allowing for the use of a number of antenna lengths. A nice set!

Paul Dennis, Tucson, AZ. "I liked the Den Two radio—suggest that the inner and outer diameters of the coil form be given. I also note that there are an odd number of slots. I think that the importance of this should be mentioned. If this design is going to the general public details are important. Basically it is an excellent design. [Editor: The author had actually included some of this information and Rebecca inadvertently deleted it before printing the last newsletter, sorry! The forms should be 4.5 in diameter and have nine 1.25 radial slots.]

George W. Hails, Arlington Heights, IL. "Phil...you asked about use of the old telephone earphones in crystal sets.... While sensitive, these were very low in impedance, about 50 to 70 ohms; hence, they loaded down sets. In the early days these earphones were much more widely available than the 2,000 ohm headsets, so they were used despite their shortcoming. The hobby magazines from 1908 - 1919 were full of warnings about the low impedance of these telco earphones, but the high Z phones finally became readily available due to World War I supply. By the way, the old Baldwin C headphone is still the all-time highest sensitivity earphone. Most people claim it is the equivalent of adding a stage of audio! My experience confirms that." [Editor. George, can you give us more detail on the Baldwins?]

VENDORS

Here are a few vendors we haven't listed before:

Play Things of Past, Gary Schneider, 9511 Sunrise Blvd #J23, Cleveland, OH 44133, (216) 251-3714. e-mail gbsptop@aol.com. Gary has a retail store in Cleveland, and a catalog of old parts and literature. The catalog includes transformers, tubes, parts, and used books and magazines, over 9800 items, it is huge. For a copy of the catalog send him $6.00, cash or check.

Ramsey Electronic Hobby and Amateur Kits, 800-446-2295. Ramsey has been around for about 20 years producing electronic kits and test equipment. John Ramsey is a member of our society so we decided to give him a listing! Most of the kits are high-tech, but we thought some of you might be intestested. Just call for a catalog.

CRYSTAL SET PROJECTS

We are winding down our Crystal Set projects contest. So if you want to get your submission in, then you have until September 30. The projects we have received have been excellent, everybody has done a great job.

If you haven't read about this before here it is: The Society will be publishing a Crystal Set Projects book this fall. Our plans are to cover projects that beginners can follow and that people can build with their children. We are also hoping to distribute this projects book to schools and clubs. We will seriously consider any project that is easy to follow and well tested. If your project is chosen for the book you will receive $50 and 5 copies of the book. Projects can be handwritten and figures hand drawn, there are no rules! Any questions call Rebecca in the office at (314) 725-1172.

INTERNET ADDRESS www.midnightscience.com
e-mail: xtalset@midnightscience.com

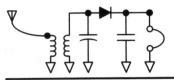

The Xtal Set Society Newsletter

| Volume 6, No. 6 | November 1, 1996 |

THE SIMPLE TRF SET
by Robert Rowe

[Editor: Due to many member's requests (more like polite demands) we are finally printing an article about the next step-up, the TRF circuit. Please write or e-mail us with your comments. A special thanks to our member Rob Rowe for taking the plunge and writing the first article.]

I've built many crystal sets over the years and have had a lot of fun with them, but my interest had slipped until I joined the Xtal Set Society a while back. After some months of playing with Xtal sets again, I began to want more performance in a simple radio circuit. This led me to begin playing with regenerative sets, which I did for a few months. One day I began thinking about TRF (Tuned Radio Frequency) receivers. Why was the TRF mentioned once in a while, but seemingly never written up as a construction idea? Guess what happened next!

The TRF in its simplest form is just two tuned circuits in series with a RF amp between the stages, followed by a detector and AF stage. In other words, a one-evening project—just my type! I got out my stack of Ken Cornell's "Radio Scrapbooks" and headed for the parts bins. After finding some AM loopsticks and a 2 x 365 pfd variable, I built a general-purpose RF amp described in the Scrapbook. I got a few more parts out and clip-leaded the whole mess together. I attached antenna and power, and was amazed at what happened! Selectivity was excellent, it was quite sensitive and audio was good. My broadcast band lash-up picked up about 25 stations one night last winter. A change of coils showed that shortwave performance below about 7 mHz was good too. This is definitely a simple radio circuit that works and sounds great!

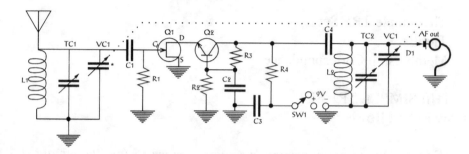

Figure 1: TRF Circuit (*dotted line denotes these two capacitors rotate from the same knob).

These plans are just a guide—like crystal sets, the TRF is a circuit type that lends itself well to tinkering. Take this basic idea and see what you can come up with! A wave trap or high-pass filter can be used ahead of the input if you have a local that overloads the receiver. Try different detector schemes; or try other types of RF amps. An audio amp/speaker (the ubiquitous Radio Shack # 277-1008) can be used at the output—fidelity is quite good. As with crystal sets, it's fun to experiment with different detectors and L/C combinations. It is interesting to note the comparatively great selectivity the TRF offers, especially when the coils are very closely duplicated and the tuning of the L/C circuits "tracks" well. Try different methods of attaching the antenna, including link-coupling it. In short, I think the TRF may be a logical step-up from XTAL sets for us, just as it was in the early days of radio.

By the way, I don't claim to be a radio design expert, and those who wish to could probably find "errors" in my sample circuit. Oh well, it works and I'm having fun and learning. I hope you do too!

Parts List

- VC1-(1) Dual 365 pfd variable (junk box, Fair Radio, etc.)
- TC1,2-(2) small trimmer capacitors (10-30 pf max) for "balancing" the tuned circuits (optional)
- L1,2-(2) RF coils (AM Loopsticks, home-made, etc.)
- D1-(1) 1N34 Diode or your choice of other type detector
- C1-(1) 220 pfd ceramic capacitor
- C2,3-(2) 0.1 mfd ceramic capacitor
- C4-(1) 0.01 mfd ceramic capacitor
- R1-(1) 1 megohm 1/4 watt resistor
- R2,3-(2) 10 k ohm 1/4 watt resistor
- R4-(1) 1 k ohm 1/4 watt resistor
- Q1-(1) MPF-102 JFET
- Q2-(1) 2N2222 NPN Transistor
- B1-(1) 9-volt battery connector, and battery
- SW1-(1) power switch, SPST type

The coils can be wound to cover the desired frequency range, depending on your variable capacitor. For starters, try 100 turns #30 wire on a 1 1/4" form for broadcast band. For shortwave try 30-50 turns and a smaller dual capacitor. The trimmers helped "peak" performance of my sample circuits. They were adjusted at both ends of the band for sharpest tuning and best tracking. The amplifier circuit is one of Ken Cornell's designs that I find to be quite useful.

TIDBITS

Jim Breeyear sent in a tip to use a potato as a solder mold for your xtal. Melt enough solder to fill hole in potato. Select a suitable galena xtal from rock specimen. Insert wire in hole. Pour solder into hole and quickly insert xtal into solder with tweezers. Remove when cool.

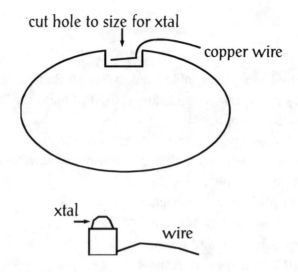

cut hole to size for xtal

copper wire

xtal → wire

Jim also sent in this safety pin as a cat whisker. Use a large safety pin with the head removed. Form a loop at the end and screw it to the board. Attach wire to loop under screw head.

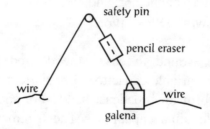

safety pin

pencil eraser

wire

wire

galena

MEMBERSHIP CORRESPONDENCE

Ian Aldridge, Sydney, Australia. "I received your books today and they are in good condition. My family won't see me for a few days while I read them! (just kidding, but my wife is beginning to fear becoming a radio widow). During my experiments I have discovered some interesting items that your readers might like to use:

"1) A good source of cat's whisker wire is old corona wire from photocopiers or laser printers; its made of tungsten and gives great contact with the crystal.

"2) I have found that series resonance tuning circuits perform very well. I have yet to determine where the detector gets enough forward bias, (probably voltage developed across the coil resistance) but the current developed at resonance drives crystal earphones to distortion. I have tested from 4 ohms up to 400 ohms with excellent results on the 400 ohm set. With more development, it may be possible to drive 8 ohm earphones. Try it! [Editor. Series resonant circuits can develop very high voltages at the point between the cap and coil. I suspect this is where your bias comes from.]

"3) If you're stuck for forms to make spider web coils, try old compact disks (CD) their dimensions and rigidity are just perfect for the job! [Editor. Ian, are you planning to cut these to make the spider? What works best to do this? Guess I'll try it on a CD I'm tired of. Neat idea!]

"4) If you have limited space for a long antenna and your home has aluminum foil-coated insulation sarking in the ceiling, then just connect your Xtal set to the sarking via an alligator clip (it's the best antenna, highest gain, I've ever used)."

Andy Catanzaro, Milwaukee, WI. "My newsletter arrived today with a renewal now sticker on it, and I wanted to write and cast a vote. Radio infested my blood in a way that was to prove lifelong when I was eight years old. The inciting vehicle was a crystal set my dad helped me make. Nevertheless, life moved on. The 2N170 and 2N707's reared their heads. Their use was unavoidable. Yet the excitement of radio was not lost. It only grew.

"You are undoubtedly aware of Charles Kitchin's definitive article, 'Regenerative Receivers' in 'Communications Quarterly,' Fall 1996. He uses modern FET technology (and even throws in a super Analog Devices op-amp in the audio section) to redefine the state of the regenerative art. Needless to say, this article has swept my attention and brought back vivid memories of the past when I was stunned at the qualities of a single transistor regenerative radio. He describes radios I can build and enjoy using the best of the new and the old.

"The 'Xtal Set Society Newsletter' could move into the valve era and still be true to original tenets: Radios that are simple, clever, and fun. There are many, many topologies to be explored and enjoyed before moving beyond Hugo Gernsback's 'Electronics for All' or Alfred Morgan's 'First Radio Book for Boys.' Even some people who are entrenched in digital radio and satellite communications can live out their original appreciation of radio with simple transistor or valve circuits.

"I will renew my subscription regardless, but want to cast a vote. You certainly will not lose any readers by expanding your repertoire of technology a little bit. The 'Xtal Set Society' name can stay the same to show the dedication to essential radio principles."

[Editor. Thanks Andy! How about a regen-reflex, a regen-FM, or...? Not sure I've ever seen a regen-reflex, but I have seen a regen-FM (in a Radio Shack multi-kit). I've noted a number of the amateur and hobby magazines "doing regen" lately. Wonder if it might somehow be related to the coming sunspot cycle? Anyway, super idea. What do the rest of you think about this?]

Ed Reinhart, Lemont, IL. "I have been a member for about 2 years now and have built a few crystal sets. I built some in boy scouts many, many years ago, and I am happy to get back into the hobby. In that I have been in electronics all my life, this really brings me back to the roots, realizing how much I forgot and really did not understand.

"I just acquired a Miller 595 tuner, it is factory built, and '595' is stamped on the variable capacitor. I really love this tuner. The selectivity is consistent throughout the band and the volume for all stations is adequate. I was amazed at the number of stations that I could receive with my 60 foot antenna and Baldwin headphones.

"Does anyone know where I can get a set of instructions for the Miller 595 tuner? It works great and is easy to tune, but I would like to have a set of instructions also."

Rick Carter, Wichita, KS. "I just received the latest issue, and when I read the story, 'Fox Hole Radio Revisited' I was reminded of a story my father told me about his first crystal radio. This would have been in the early thirties. My dad enlisted the aid of his father in collecting materials for the radio. I don't know where he got the plans, but when it came time for the earphones my grandfather came home with the handset from a telephone. It worked great. My father would hook it up to his crystal set, and lay it on his pillow at night and listen to KFH here in Wichita (when he was supposed to be going to sleep for school the next day).

"While experimenting with my recently built crystal set I came across the guts from an old telephone handset and hooked it up with the alligator clips. It works as good as my vintage headphones. I enjoy the newsletter very much and thought I would share this story." [Thanks! Ed.]

Jim Christensen, Duluth, MN. "My first love is to make things and have them work. I used to have (when I was 12 up on the iron range) an old galena crystal which was set in a lead piece. This all went into a holder with a cat whisker 'tickler' and an old pair of 2,000 ohm earphones without pads! After a session my ears would really hurt, but I didn't care. I had all the wire I could ever find strung up out in the trees. Boy the thrill when the catwisker found a hot spot on the crystal. I have all manner of radio's now—shortwave receivers, ham stuff, you name it—but my fondest memories are as a boy looking out the north upstairs window and listening to KXEL from Waterloo, IA." [Editor. Jim, I've heard it said that the Minnesota iron range "sucks up" radio signals—just makes 'em disappear. What's the deal? Old wive's tale? My folks came from Duluth and I remember a bit about the place...snow.]

Stanley Garber, Elkhart, IN. "I wanted to tell you how much I enjoy your newsletter and other publications. I first started playing with xtal sets as a kid. Now in my 40s I enjoy rediscovering the simplicity of their design and performance. Keep up the good work!"

Nicholas Dudisch, Ilion, NY. "My first crystal radio was a Philmore. I lived on a farm without any electricity and spent some of the evenings listening to WGY in Schenectady, NY, about 60 miles away. The antenna was a vertical about 50 feet long. I retired from being a school teacher in a vocational school. I taught electronics. One of the projects that the first month's students had to build was a crystal radio using a germanium diode. Usually they were able to pick up some stations located about a 30 mile radius. The thrill of actually building and listening to their radio project was a pleasure to behold."

Ned Ely, Alvin, TX. "I haven't corresponded in a while but read the issues with interest and enjoyment. The enclosed article ("The Design and Construction of R.F. Coils," by Herbert Brier, Radio & TV News, August '56) has worked great for me in cook-booking different inductors." [Editor. Here's a quote on Q from the article. "Coil efficiency is determined by the ratio of inductive reactance to its losses (R). It is difficult to predict beforehand (true)! However, experimental work has established a few factors that produce a high Q coil: fairly large diameter, length not appreciably less than half diameter, largest solid wire (that accommodates inductance needed)...and Q varies approximately as the square of the diameter."]

Kevin Norton, Weymouth, MA. Kevin sent us a note following the last issue and makes a very good point, "The strong point of Radio Shack crystal sets comes from the fact that they are so inexpensive and readily available (additional parts for modifications too)."

[Editor. Kevin. You're absolutely right. I think we tend to forget what a super source RS is for crystal parts. You mentioned earlier that some kits (perhaps because they've been in the catalog so long) seem to cost less than the sum we'd pay for all the parts today!]

Bob Foster. Greensboro NC. "I've been enjoying the xtal set newsletter...I wait eagerly the submissions to your Xtal Set Project competition. Keep up the good work!" [Editor. Thanks Bob. The Crystal Set Projects book will be super fun with a wide variety of sets! Regarding Literary Digest, I still have some of the old articles on file but the "powers to be" haven't granted me 26 hours per day instead of 24 which would be neat...maybe this winter I can dig into them and others!]

Jean Doksansky, Fremont, NE, [Editor. Jean just sent me a very interesting article about Edwin Armstrong's inventions, titled "Radio Revolutionary," published in Invention and Technology, Fall, 1985, Volume 1, Number 2. "Edwin Armstrong's innovations culminated in the introduction of FM...." I didn't know this magazine existed but am very excited to find out about it. Innovation history is an exciting topic. Jean noted that he'd gotten a copy from his local library, so perhaps others will be just as lucky. Jean, can you send us an address for the magazine and we'll print it in the next issue. I noted that GM sponsors it.]

Dick Mackiewicz, Coventry, CT. "Phil, here are some potential answers to some questions posed in the newsletter. Possible source for German Silver Wire is a good jeweler. The RADAK was made by Clapp Eastham, 136 Main St., Cambridge, MA about 1923. I have been collecting earphones for many years and have several sets of Baldwins (with mica, fibre, and aluminum diaphragms). The Baldwins operate on a unique 'balanced armature' principle. Nathanial Baldwin of Salt Lake City, Utah patented these phones in the early 1900s. The mica diaphragm units are the most sought after. See 'Construction and Action of a Loudspeaker Unit,' by J.E. Anderson, for an explanation of the 'action' of Baldwin phones,

Radio World, April 24th, 1926." [Editor. Dick, thanks for the very fine correspondence! Phones continue to be a very interesting topic.]

Editor. Dick also sent us a photo of a Tikker wheel he recently obtained. Thanks! I'd really like to find a Tikker set for my collection. I describe this "first of the digital radios" in my Crystal Set Handbook, Vol III., page 44. The Tikker is the forerunner of what is happening today in radio design; microcomputer chips are taking over portions of new designs, performing intermediate frequency (IF) and detection processing with programming! Would anyone find an article titled "From Crystal Set to Computer-based Radios interesting?

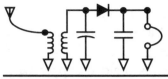

The Xtal Set Society Newsletter

Volume 7, No. 1   January 1, 1997

IN THIS ISSUE (#34) January 1, 1997

MEMBERSHIP CORRESPONDENCE

Rob Mott, Lewisburg, WV. Rob had written in earlier about testing his radios in the "Quiet Zone," but we didn't know what the heck that was! Rob wrote back with more info, "The 'Quiet Zone' is the area of closely supervised RF admissions to protect the radio astronomy obervatory at Green Bank, WV from QRM, even at this distance (about 50 M) we still have to have frequency coordination and release for our agencies uhf system before we can get it installed. I had the opportunity to test one of my sets on a camping trip in the 'Quiet Zone' for the National Radio Observatory. I took a variation of the set from Volume 4, No. 6 of the newsletter (with multiple switched detectors). In general the set was quite impressive. Daytime and nighttime reception of WRON (1KW), about 45 miles south of the camp was excellent, yet at that distance it didn't overwhelm the entire band, allowing the reception of more distant stations. I suspect the setting was similar to that of xtal set users in the 20's and 30's, no nearby stations and few, if any, clear channel stations. Also with "tapping up" the cap, crystal (1N34 and a galena detector), antenna and ground, I was able to tune in RCI, BBC, and an unidentified Chinese language station. Pretty flexible rig!"

Henry "Hank" Alcott, Chino Valley, AZ. "As a youngster, I built several crystal sets using this simple design. We lived about 25 miles from Boston and WBZ, one of the original 50,000 Watt radio stations in the nation. That, no doubt, had a lot to do with why it worked. We didn't have plumbing, so the ground was a piece of pipe driven into the ground. The antenna was braided copper wire strung between two glass insulators, and it was about 40 feet long - strung between the house and a tree. The crystal was quite large, about 3/8", and was set in lead in a brass pan about 3/4" in diameter. The "cat whisker" was a safety pin with a loop to fit under a small bolt for a connection. Later on I was given a commercially built set that was in a wooden box about 6" x 6" square, and 6" high. This unit had a tuning coil 2 1/2" x 5" inside the box. The set looked a lot neater, but it never did work as well as the simple home made set. I've been enjoying your newsletter. You get some really good ideas to play with. Some of my grandkids will probably get exposed to crystal radio about Christmas time!"

George Trudeau, Sandwich, MA. "I recently built the Quaker Oats box set that you have plans for on your web site (Editor: also printed in the Crystal Set Handbook). It works fine even though there are no local AM stations here in Sandwich on Cape Cod. I connected it to my ham radio mulitband vertical and the first station I heard was Christian Science Monitor broadcasting on shortwave—I think from Cutler, Maine on 6 Mhz! The only deviation from the plans was I used a Quaker Corn Meal box instead of Oats. Is this why it gets short-wave? At night I mostly get WTOP in Washington, DC. The most interesting part of it was I brought it to work to show to the people I work with. They were completely baffled. They had never seen such a thing, and could not conceive that it was a radio. I see wire, and these look like headphones, but where's the radio!" [Editor. You're north of the 39th parallel so that's why you get HF, but only on April 1. Nice story! Modern folk don't have a clue, do they! Ask a teenager who Truman was. Then again ask anybody over 50 who Madonna is—the singer that is!]

John Cich, internet. "The latest set built in the house was by my 12 year old. She took second place in her school's science fair in May, with a variation of the basic set outlined in the Crystal Set

Handbook. She used a Morton salt box core and a shoebox base. Last xmas I did a simple single coil slider as a present for my brother and his wife. On a slice of oak from the wood pile, stained and finished, the 'sliding arm' was one of those blank board slot covers you have left over when you install pc boards on your personal computer. It was a big hit at his holiday party. I have a pocket set I did about 10 years ago, really Radio Shack's cardboard kit built into one of their smallest blue kit boxes. My first kit was a birthday gift from my dad when I was 12, a remco gray plastic futuristic looking rig with a real rock in it. I still use the Superex headset he bought to go with it!"

Rob Meloy, Wlfd, Conneticut. "Just a few ideas I have found helpful for those who can't find galena. I have found that Iron Pyrite (fools gold) is supurb and much more available. Also, Radio Shack sells a package of assorted chokes and coils. In using small slug tuned coils in place of a regular coil I have had some very good DX on shortwave. It takes some experimenting but its worth the trial and error. Besides anyone can DX with a commercial set, but there is nothing like hearing Radio Japan on a rock!" [We agree!]

David Krucas, San Diego, CA. "Thank you for publishing my comments on testing headphones using dental fillings in the September issue. A couple weeks after the issue came out, I was in an antique store when I found a decent pair of headphones. The only trouble was that they had a quarter-inch phone plug attached. I put the plug in my mouth with the tip on a molar filling while I tried to curl my tongue up to the ring. After half a minute a trying, a couple of women walked by me, and yes, they were staring. I tried to say "it's an old radio trick," but I doubt they believed it. I enjoy collecting old things and thinking about what daily life would have been like during my parents or grandparents days. My crystal radio gets my imagination going."

Donald Powers, internet. "I am 53 years old, and I remember a small radio offered on the back of a cereal box, I think Cheerios. This would have been in the 50's. I think the radio was small, approximately 1 inch square at the bottom, about 2½ inches tall, tapering down at the top to about ½ inch, with a small brass ball connected to a brass shaft that you pulled up or down, in and out of the base, to find a station. It had only an ear plug to listen from and I think it was tan in color. Does anyone else remember this radio? I guess I could be nuts and it maybe never existed!"

Merlin Kallinen, Silver Bay, MN. "Having just read two of Phil's xtal books, I decided to write. Presently, I am 64 years old and just retired in May. When I was a kid I used to play around with crystal sets and one tubers. Since last summer I have begun building and experimenting with crystal sets once again. I have been winding coils until I can't see straight. Try as I might, my sets with cylindrical coils were at best mediocre in performance. Then I started making spider web coils using plastic up to $1/_8$ inch thick, and wound tapped coils on forms up to 5½ inches in diameter, with 17 inch spokes. I presently have a set with a coil about 3" diameter, and 62 turns of #28 enamel wire. It has 9 taps, 5 turns apart on the first 45 turns from the center. I used a simple "basic" hook-up on this one, except for one thing...I used (2) 1N34A diodes in parallel, and just before I started this letter I picked up Montreal on it! I have also received Winnipeg, International Falls, Des Moines, and the local Minneapolis-St. Paul stations. I live about 350 yards from Lake Superior, but we are surrounded by very high hills on 3 sides. I didn't have a high impedance audio XFRMR, and so, after some thought, I tried on old car ignition coil that had about 10,300 ohms on the hi-voltage side on my Fluke 77 meter.. It works!" [Editor. You mean you attached a speaker, using the car coil to match the 8-ohm speaker? Cool!]

Tom Carlson, Mound MN. "Where can one obtain a 10μa analog microammeter for use as a tuning aid and/or signal strength meter as mentioned by David Wasson in the May 1994 newsletter? I use a 25μa meter, obtained from a hamfest but would like a smaller scale, does anyone know if they are even made anymore?"

Jack Gardner, Anaheim, CA. "About a month ago I sent you some diode characteristic curves but at the time I didn't include galena. Here's a set with galena."

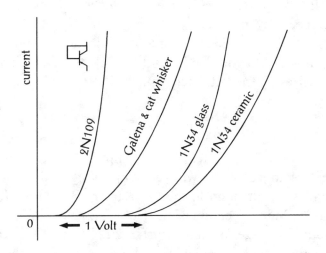

Figure 2: Diode characteristic curves

"The transistor as diode exhibited the best threshold value, the forward applied bias (voltage) at which the diode begins to conduct (flow current). The PNP transistor is configured (wired) as a two-lead diode by tying the base and collector together. The galena and cat whisker rectifier was a close second, so we can see why it was so popular in the 1920s. The "standard," once glass diodes appeared, was (and still is) the 1N34. I've not shown a 1N914 silicon diode but it's threshold would be about 7 volts, much higher than those shown. The curves were taken using a curve tracer with the headphones replaced by a 2,000 ohm carbon resistor. Many tests were made adjusting the cat whisker to find the best demodulation action for the galena sample."

[Editor. All of the curves give the same "shape." Marconi's early radios often used Carborundum, and it's threshold voltage is about 2 volts. He "assisted" the carborundum by applying a bias voltage, obtained by using a 4 V battery and potentiometer. Here's what Elmer Bucher says about the arrangement (Practical Wireless

Telegraphy, page 135, 1917), " The application of a weak battery current to the carborundum crystal and head telephone circuit has been found to have a marked effect on the intensity of the incoming signals." By the way, some copies of Bucher's book can still be found in specialty bookstores such as Rain Day Books[1] in New Hampshire. Jack, why don't you rerun your curves with a bias of about 1 volt added to your diodes with a 100K or 1 Megohm resistor added in series. I tried it once with a 1N914 and got increased sensitivity.]

Frederick W. Chesson, Waterbury, CT. "What has your society learned about the interesting attempts by inventors and experimenters to come up with an amplifying and/or oscillating xtal? I call your attention to the Old Timers Bulletin[2], November 1996 page 10. In it, a mention is made of a US patent of 1923 by one C.G. Smith for a germanium crystal amplifier. Were any such devices commercially available? Were they "bought up" or otherwise quashed by "the big radio-tube makers" or were they too far ahead of the technology of the time for economical and reliable production?" [Editor. Oscillating crystals were mentioned frequently in articles about Pickard, who experimented with fused silicon detectors in 1906. Tunnel diodes evolved later commercially. I suspect you are right; the concept was ahead of its time. Would be interesting to follow up on this. A parallel, the 100 mile/gallon carburetor, did it exist, was is buried by gas and oil interests?]

L. Gardener, Tonawanda, NY. A note on Vol 6, No. 5. "John's crystal set is excellent. I've used it many times. It can be improved immensely if the coils are made of LITZ wire wound on a powdered iron core. Second, remove the bypass on the detector and place it across the phones."

Jim Trent, Lexington Park, MD. "Just a note as a new member to thank you for your effort in publishing the newsletters and books related to xtal sets. My sample newsletter I received from a request to your web site sold me. My previous experience with xtal sets was back in the early 40s when I purchased my Philmore Crystal Radio from the old Johnson Smith catalog." [Editor. Jim sent along a note on an error in a coil formula in my CRYSTAL SET HANDBOOK. Jim, you are right. If we reprint, which is likely, I'll make the necessary modifications. Thanks!]

[1]Rainy Day Books, Box 775, Fitzwilliam, NH 03447-0775 (603) 585-3448

[2]The Old Timer's Bulletin, Official Journal of the Antique Wireless Association, Inc. Box E Breesport, NY 14816. Published 4 times a year for the members of the AWA. The AWA is a nonprofit historical society founded in 1952. Dues $15/year.

GERMAN SILVER WIRE

Joe Gougon, Oscar, LA. "In September's correspondence, Jim Shattuck asked about German silver wire. I don't know if he can use it, but flat German silver wire for gunstock inlay is available from Dixie Gun Works, Inc., Gunpower Lane, Union City, TN 38261, phone 901-885-0700, order line 800-238-6785. The dimensions are 0.008 by 0.1 inches, cat # IP03031 $ 3.50/yard. Their catalog says that German Silver is 55% copper, 25% zinc, and 20% nickle." [Editor. Goodies like this are super welcome. Our stuff can sometimes be hard to find. Thanks again Joe.]

Jim Schlaf, Clearwater, FL. More on German Silver! "German Silver is an old fashioned term for nickel-chromium. It somewhat resembles silver in appearance but does not tarnish and was therefore used for ornamental and decorative purposes in lieu of real silver. The modern equivalent is known as "Nichrome" wire. It can be any one of several alloys of nickel and chrome that have high electrical resistance. Due to this property, Nichrome is used in the heating coils of electrical appliances. It may also be found in wire-wound thermostats and resistors. Also, many home heating thermostats contain a small, thin piece of Nichrome wire that is known as the "heat anticipator" in the HVAC trade. It might be just right for a cat whisker." [Editor. WOW. Neat! By the way, this is reminiscent of the name change from wireless to radio and then back to wireless. In Marconi's time they called what we do "wireless." Once AM radio came on it was RADIO. Today in commercial two-way, we're all of a sudden calling it wireless again. I know about nichrome wire but never equated it with German silver!]

CRYSTAL SET PROJECTS CONTEST

We didn't finish the CRYSTAL SET PROJECTS book in time to announce it in this issue. However, it has been produced and we are editing quickly. We will announce its availability as soon as it is back from the printer (We hope that will be before the March newsletter!) We will also list the winners in the newsletter.

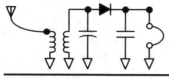

The Xtal Set Society Newsletter

Volume 7, No. 2   March 1, 1997

IN THIS ISSUE (#35) MARCH 1, 1997

FLAME DETECTOR FOR THE XTAL SET
by Nile Steiner

Larry Hall called me the other day to report that he and his brother Jed had made a detector first using an acetylene flame and then using a flame from an ordinary propane torch.

Larry had previously been experimenting with a flame speaker where sound comes from a flame driven with a high voltage audio signal. I had always thought that high voltages were always necessary in order to get any appreciable current to flow through a flame of any kind. That all changed when Larry told me that he had made an Xtal set detector.

I tried the same experiment here in California and got essentially the same results. I also experimented with the flame's conductivity and resistance. I would like, in the near future, to set up a curve tracer again and get some curves.

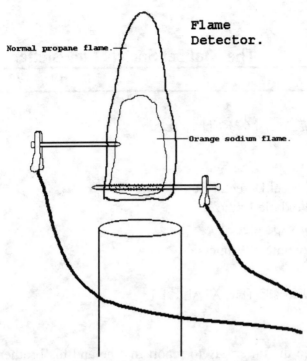

Figure 1: Flame detector

The letter from Larry is as follows:

"I think any crystal radio layout would work with the flame detector in place of the crystal or diode. The flame detector doesn't work as well as a crystal but it does work well enough to hear a strong station. I first tried an oxy-acetylene torch and tungsten rods and got good results. Then I tried the following: Use a common propane torch and two 1/16 dia. steel welding rods about 4 inches long (my welding rod is copper coated). Adjust the propane flame up enough to be able to make the ends of the rods red hot but not up so high as to make a lot of noise. Hold the rods with test leads and connect in place of the diode. Heat one rod red hot on the end (1/4 inch or so) and then plunge it into some common table salt. Put back into the flame with the other rod and experiment with position in the flame—it seems critical. Put one rod above the other; the salted rod on the bottom near the edge of the propane flame and the other rod on the edge of the bright orange (ionized) tail from the salted lower rod. The rods can be anywhere from 1/16" to 1/2" or more apart."

When I tried the same experiment here, I used a couple of finishing nails instead of welding rod. The xtal set circuit that I used was a garden variety antenna tapped into the coil of an LC circuit feeding a detector and crystal earphone.

The detector worked best with the nails in the same position as described above by Larry. That is, having the salted nail much in the bottom of the flame and the tip of the other nail further up, about 1/16 inch into the orange flame. The intensity of the orange flame starts to diminish after a minute or so and the nail needs to be re-salted.

I found that the flame detector works best after the nail has been salted several times and a lot of black burned salt crud has built up on it. Both nails need to be hot. The bottom salted nail must be red hot whereas the upper nail only needs to be somewhat hot.

In testing the flame device electrically, it seemed to act like a resistor that has much more resistance in one direction than the other. The lower salted nail seems to be the cathode (-) and the upper nail, the anode (+). With 12vdc applied, I could get 10 microamperes to flow in one direction and 40 microamperes to flow in the other. This calculated out to be approximately 1.2 M ohms reverse resistance and approximately 300 K ohms forward resistance.

An ordinary ohmmeter, using a 1.5 volt battery, was then connected across the flame device. The lowest forward resistance reading was approximately 70 K ohm and the lowest reverse resistance reading was approximately 200 K ohm. I seemed to get a somewhat lower forward resistance reading (approximately 40 K ohm) when the upper nail was substituted with a pin. These high resistance values would seem to indicate that the best performance in a xtal set would be when driving a very high impedance earphone or amp. The crystal earphone used here fills that requirement.

Some of the questions that arise are:

1. What kind of resistance vs. voltage curve does this thing have?
2. Does the current flow instantaneously through the flame or does it travel slowly, from a dependence upon the moving flame to carry the electrons or ions? Running a pulse through it and watching with an oscilloscope could answer this one.

3. Is there any kind of negative resistance?

4. Could it even possibly act in a way similar to a vacuum tube triode by putting a grid between the cathode and anode?

I plan to do some more experimenting and hope to be able to give a future second report on the flame detector.

THE CARBON AND STEEL DETECTOR SET, AKA "THE FOXHOLE RADIO"
by Phil Anderson, WØXI

A number of articles appeared in the forties and fifties about GIs making "foxhole" radios. Legend has it that these sets used a razor blade and a lead pencil detector. I recall reading a few of these articles while browsing in the library archives. One has to wonder though, and I don't recall reading, what kind of headphones they had? It's likely that these were "procured" from the supply depot, or perhaps they used "field phones." Wire would not have been a problem; one could have easily pulled a generator or alternator out of a dead vehicle and unwound the wire! Simple enough.

So what did these foxhole radios consist of anyway? Without a tunable capacitor they contained just five parts; the antenna, and antenna coil, a razor blade, a lead pencil, and a pair of headphones (or one headphone). To work well, the coil had to have the right number of turns and the right diameter and wire spacing to "match" the capacitance of the wire antenna, and the wire antenna had to be (and usually was) less than a quarter wavelength of the frequency of reception. With this configuration, shown in Figure 2, the capacitance of the (short) antenna combined with the inductance of the antenna coil, create a large voltage at their connecting point. This large voltage makes it possible for the less-than-ideal carbon and steel detector to function.

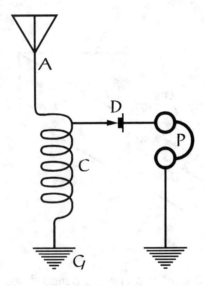

Figure 2: Fox-hole set; *A*=antenna 75 feet, *C*=coil 80 turns, *D*=diode, *G*=ground, *P*=earphones

No doubt this "theory" was unknown to many who built these sets, but they succeeded by trial and error anyway. You can recreate this scene by winding about 80 closely wound turns (#24 to #30 plastic coated wire) on a piece of two by four. Make eyelets about every five turns so you can experiment with tuning the antenna with the right length of coil. String up about 75 feet of wire for the antenna. Since this is less than a quarter wavelength anywhere in the broadcast band, the antenna will be capacitive and match your coil. Get the antenna as high as possible above the ground.

How do you wire up the carbon and steel detector? Clip a wire from the coil to one end of the blade and fashion a holder to apply the pencil lead against either flat outer edge of the blade. Whittle off the eraser end of the pencil so that you can clip a wire to the carbon (or lead) center to go to the headphones. Attach the other end of the headphones to ground and to the base of the antenna coil. Your challenge will be to fashion a holder for the pencil so that it can be pressed against the blade with just the right amount of pressure. I've found that too little or too much pressure will not cut it. A light pressure seems to be what's needed.

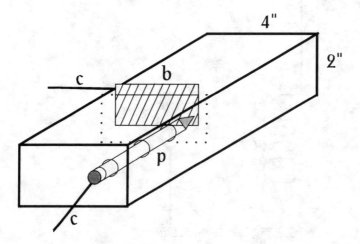

Figure 3: Simple holder for razor and pencil detector; b=razor blade, p=pencil, c=clip leads

You can build a simple "holder" for the pencil and blade out of a piece of two by four if you have a saw and drill (see figure 3). Cut a slit in the two by four about two thirds of the way through and about an inch from the end. Then drill a hole that is a tight but workable fit for the pencil and push it in until it hits the blade. Twist the pencil to apply just the right amount of pressure. I sometimes found the sweet spot by tapping the pencil once it was pressing against the blade. It takes a bit of work and is reminiscent of trying to find that sweet spot on a piece of galena crystal with a cat whisker (fine steel wire).

How does the carbon and pencil detector compare? This detector is not as sensitive as a 1N34 or a galena and catwhisker detector. It works about as well as a carborundum detector, like those used in early Marconi sets. From my experience "blue" blades seem to work the best, but any clean blade will do.

Marconi found that application of a weak battery current to the carborundum crystal and headphone circuit (in one direction only) had a marked effect on the intensity of the incoming signals. So, if you live in an area that doesn't have a super strong station, but perhaps a station that delivers a moderate signal to your location, you might wish to try the circuit shown in Figure 4. Adjust the potentiometer for maximum signal reception.

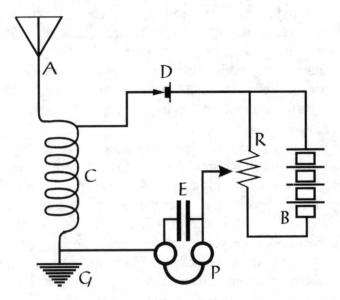

Figure 4: Battery boosted reception; *A*=antenna 75 feet, *C*=Coil 80 turns, *D*=diode, *G*=ground, *E*=capacitor .01 mfd, *R*=resistor 100K pot, *B*=4 volt battery, *P*=earphones

Membership Correspondence

Vic Spicer, Winnipeg, Manitoba. "I wanted to make a set with enough selectivity to pick out our two cbc stations, English and French sitting at 990 kHz and 1050 kHz respectively. The set is built on a 8" x 8" piece of oak, formerly a 'foxes and geese' game board.

All connections are done with brass screws and nuts; headphones are also vintage. The antenna and detector circuits are identical, each with a 40-400 pf air-spaced metal variable capacitor cannibalized out of an old tube radio. The inductors consist of 45 turns of #24 wire on a 2.5" OD form made of PVC drain pipe, with taps at every 5 turns. The inductance is measured to be about 170 μH, giving a frequency range of 610-1930 kHz. The antenna is about 20 meters of #22 wire strung along the back fence. Inductors L1 and L2 sit about 2" apart. When both capacitors are set to resonance, the signal strength rises sharply. It almost makes tuning a challenge, as both C1 and C2 suffer from picking up hand capacitance."

Vic also wrote us on e-mail describing another set he was working on. "I am really getting into this crystal set stuff! After some tinkering, I've come up with a kind of recreation of Pickard's 1902 detector. It's a 3H pencil lead wrapped/soldered to a mangled safety pin, pressing down on a rusted iron disc about the size of a penny. When properly adjusted performance is quite good, getting all our local AM stations strong and clear. The drawbacks, of course, are that it's mechanically and electrically very fragile, bump the table and the set is on. Last night the static from touching one of the cats wiped out a big section of sensitive oxide layer, so I had to flip the disc over and use the other side. A big thanks to Phil Kinzie for his excellent reference, *Crystal Radio: History, Fundamentals, and Design*."

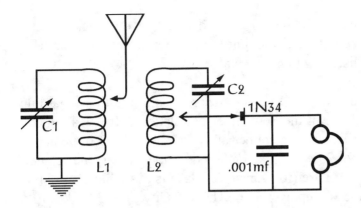

Figure 5: Vic's 'Foxes and Geese' radio schematic

Nick Leggett, Reston, VA. "I am a new member responding to a letter to the editor that suggested that the scope of the Society should be increased. I think the Society should remain focused primarily on crystal sets. Some articles on simple vacuum tube and transistor regenerative or TRF receivers are fine. No integrated circuits, and no gee-whiz articles about the wonders of high tech. Please retain your focus on the elegance of SIMPLE electronic design. Please tell the author, Phil Kinzie, that his book on crystal set history and design is excellent."

Steve Galchutt, Colorado Springs, CO. "I'm a QRP (low power) ham radio buff and always have been active in building little portable gear for backpacking. Seeing the crystal set homepage reminded me of my youth. My older brother gave a crystal set kit that I built with his help of course, and for days I walked around clipping onto anything that was metal, cars, fences, light posts, even my dog's tail. Looking for the best antenna (reception), I finally strung a piece of rusty old barbed wire I found to the tree house. It became my first ham shack. I spent hours in it with my friends listening to that ear piece. It was an old hearing-aid style, singe sided with a wooden handle...like the one used by a hearing impaired lady who sat one row in front of us in church. I often wondered if she really was listening to the boring sermon or KFI radio. After awhile the crabby neighbor lady complained that the tree house was an eyesore and down it came, wire and all! Later, I strung another wire from my bedroom window to the old oak tree out back (former home of the tree house...I thought the tree was a receptor for RF!) and continued listening to my crystal set."

Bob Zinck, Halifax, NS Canada. "There was a question regarding German Silver wire in the September newsletter. My 1914 general chemistry book lists it as a copper alloy: Copper—50-60%, Zinc—20%, Nickle—20-25%." As mentioned in the January newsletter, flat German-silver wire (for gunstock inlay) is available from Dixie Gun Works, Inc. Gunpower Lane, Union City, TN 38261, (901) 885-0700.

Peter Demmer, Aiea, HI. "Yes, over the course of 55 years, I have built several sets. Ah yes, the fine thread to my youth. Over the galactic cross-roads that salted the earth with galena. Through the vacuum of the time of thoriated tungsten, whence we have traveled. Now, we have entered from the doorway of lead pyrites (galena), and went marching across the mounds of doped germanium behind us. Does not the overwhelming evidence of silicon substracts around our feet speak so very well. Have we not come full circle in this our footprints upon the vapor deposited silicon of sand."

Bill McBride, Ferndale, CA. "Until a couple of weeks ago, I had not built a crystal set in many years, but I have fond memories of the many sets that I built as a boy. The set I remember most was built with two shotgun shells, one 12 gauge and one 20 gauge each with a coil of maybe 30 gauge wire closely wound around them. It was tuned by sliding the smaller coil into and out of the larger coil. A diode was the detector and it was carried around in my pocket most of the time. It only covered half of the band, but was a lot of fun anyhow. Although I now understand all of the theory, that was such a mystery to me as a boy, I have never lost my enthusiasm for crystal radios. I helped my son build a crystal set a couple of weeks ago and it inspired me to look on the internet to see what information was available."

John Schroeder, Beaverton, OR. John sent in the name of a vendor that carries 99.99% pure silver wire. 26 gauge is $1.05/ft! Wavetrace Technologies, 122 S. Clearwater/Largo Rd. Largo, FL 33770. (813) 587-7868

XTAL SET PROJECT CONTEST WINNERS

The projects book is almost complete, and we will be able to ship it before the next newsletter is published. If you would like a copy before the next newsletter, just check our web site in about a month or call and leave Rebecca a voice mail message. This is it guys, here are the winners! They are listed in order of appearance in the book.

Low Budget Xtal Set, William Simes
A Loop Antenna Crystal Set, Michael Mauser
Benjamin and David Goldenberg's Very-Fine
   Old-Time Crystal Radio, Benjamin and David Goldenberg
The Directional Loop DX Xtal Set, Joseph Cooper
The Den Two Crystal Radio, Alan R. Klase
How to Build and Use a High Performance Crystal Set, Lance
   Borden
A Homemade Variable Capacitor and a Trap Tuned Set, Eric
   Hudson
Build a Matchbox Crystal Radio, Jim Clark
A Krystal Kludge, William Simes
A Triple Tuned Crystal Set, Greg Constant
My Best Set Yet, Carl Davis
Yesterday's Circuit Today's Parts, William Simes
A Magic Coil for Crystal Radios, George Hails
Antenna-Ground System, Mark Zechar
The Design and Construction of a Ferrite Loopstick Inductor for an
   AM Broadcast Receiver, Ross Wollrab

Thanks to everyone who participated in this contest!

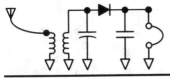

The Xtal Set Society Newsletter

Volume 7, No. 3   May 1, 1997

IN THIS ISSUE (#36) MAY 1, 1997

TRF Receiver, Using the ZN414

by Bob Flick

[Editor. Bob sent us a nice construction layout and schematic for a ZN414-based tuned radio frequency (TRF) receiver. Since we'd planned to feature "one tubers" from time to time, this modern day TRF seemed like a good spot to start. Take away the integrated circuit (IC) and the earpiece audio amp and this set is left with the components of a typical crystal set, less the detector.

The Ferranti ZN414 is a ten transistor tuned radio frequency (TRF) circuit packaged in a 3-pin TO-18 transistor package for simplicity and space economy. The circuit provides a complete RF amplifier, AM detector, and automatic gain control (AGC) circuit while requiring only six external parts to give a high quality AM tuner.

This "IC" is the basis for Bob's circuit reported below. Bob purchased his ZN414 samples from DC Electronics (address in vendor section). Although this device may not always be available, undoubtedly similar chips are available on the market...members, lease report in on sources for this part or similar parts. This part looks excellent as a TRF-based radio building block.]

The ZN414, our first active part (Q1), consists of a few stages of RF amplification and an AM detector. It's packaged as if it were a transistor, having just three leads: input, ground, and output. The output doubles as the supply point of the device; power is applied via R2 (1K). Presumably, the device is biased by R1 (100K) via coupling coil L3. The output of the ZN414 is AC-coupled to our second active device, Q2, an NPN transistor. Q2 amplifies the audio detected by the ZN414 to drive the earphones. You could add a 1K to 8 ohm transformer here if you want to drive a small 8 ohm speaker.

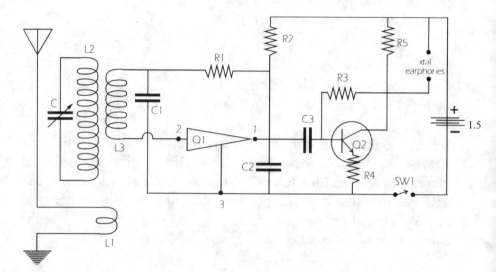

Figure 1: Schematic for the ZN414 receiver

The rest of the set consists of a batch of resistors, a switch (optional), the coils and caps necessary for the input of the radio, and the usual crystal set parts. All of the resistors can be 1/4-watt, and Q2 can be any small signal NPN transistor, such as a Radio Shack #276-2009, a PN-2222, or a 2N-2222.

Table 1: Bill of Materials

C	365 pf	R3	100K
C1	0.01 µf	R4	270 Ω
C2	0.1 µf	R5	10K
C3	0.1 µf	Q1	ZN414
R1	100K	Q2	276-2009 Radio Shack
R2	1K	Switch	s.p.s.t.

Figure 2, Construction PCB Plan, also supplied by Bob, shows us how he constructed his set. He took a small piece of copper-clad printed circuit board (which you can get from Radio Shack, including etching solution and masking marker pen), laid out rectangular areas on it to solder to, drilled a few holes, etched the pcb, and then simply solder-tacked on the components. Nice technique.

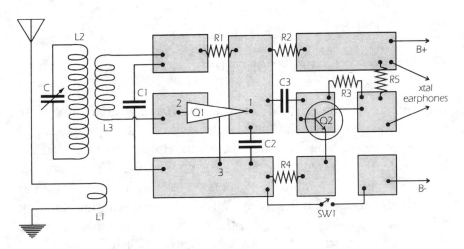

Figure 2: Construction PCB Plan

Bob's bill-of-materials for the set is shown in Table 1. He doesn't list the xtal earphone, but be sure to use the high impedance type (10K or so), which you can order from Mouser (or other sources). All capacitors, resistors, and Q2 should be obtainable from Digi-Key, Mouser, or Radio Shack.

Details on the coils are listed in Table 2. These coils are to be wound on a 4 inch by 3/8th inch ferrite rod made of #61 ferrite material. It's likely that any old transistor rod will work well too; experiment. Wind the antenna pickup coil (L1) at the bottom of the rod; wind the main tuning coil (L2) in the middle of the rod; and wind the circuit pickup coil, L3, in the middle and on top of L2.

Regarding antennas Bob writes, "Use an indoor antenna, 10-20 feet long for local stations. For nighttime use, use an outdoor antenna [for DX signals]."

Table 2: Coils, wound on a ferrite rod of #61 material. Use # 22 to # 26 wire.

coil	for	# turns
L1	antenna	1 or 2
L2	main coil	41
L3	pick-up coil	7

MEMBERSHIP CORRESPONDENCE

Bill Mitch, Hebron, IN, N9JTR. "I was reading about Fox Hole radios & German Silver in the March issue.... About 50 years ago my father showed me how to make a Fox Hole radio. We tried the blue blade, the thin red blade, and a rusty razor blade. The rusty one worked the best with more "hot" spots on it. We picked up WLS out of Chicago, about 40 miles away. When I worked with my father in the tool & die business, we used flat German silver for springs; we popped stamped parts out of a die with them. 73s. Bill."

Bill McGraw, Greenville, MS. Bill has the Society's <u>Crystal Set Handbook</u> and had some questions.

Question #1: "Page 68...when you say quarter-wavelength....a quarter of what?" [Editor. I peeked at the handbook and that section has to do with wire antennas for HF listening, i.e. DXing. What I meant was to cut an antenna to one-quarter wavelength corresponding to the frequency you would be receiving on. As I sometimes do, I listed the derived formula without explaining where it came from! Stop that! Basically, the wavelength of a radio signal is inversely proportional to it's frequency, and the proportionality constant is the speed of light. In formula form this is written as, wavelength = speed of light / frequency, where wavelength is in meters, the frequency is in Megahertz, and the speed of light is 300 million meters/second, the constant. I derived the formula on page 68 by converting the above formula into feet and dividing by four. One-quarter wavelength of antenna is ideal for crystal set use in that it presents a resistive load to the radio set and also allows the antenna to be selective, thereby helping the set to be selective.]

Question #2: "If the frequency range is the entire AM broadcast band, how do you determine the antenna length?" [Editor. Super question! One must compromise. Cut the antenna for the part of the band you listen in; or cut it for the middle of the band; or put up several antennas. Alternatively, add some L and C (coil and capacitor) at the input to the set to "tune the antenna" for each portion of the band. The problem is that one must adapt the antenna and receiver for a three to one frequency range: 550 kHz to 1600 kHz. If you're going to have just one antenna, cut it for a quarter wavelength at 1650 kHz, the "top" of the AM band; this way, the antenna will always be equal to or less than a quarter wavelength— and one can add coil inductance only at the set to tune the antenna.]

Question #3: "If steel or aluminum were substituted for copper, how does this affect the formulas for inductance?" [Editor. Not much! However, the "Q" or quality factor of the coil is affected, and this is important at the higher frequencies. Q, a measure of resistive (heat) losses in the coil, effect the selectivity of a set in that the resistance is increased as the frequency is in-creased. Definitely use copper for HF DXing sets.]

Question #4: "Is there a formula to determine mil diameter from the AWG wire size?" [Editor. I'm not sure. You could plot the table on page 121 of the <u>Handbook</u> and then generate your own formula from the following:

$Y = mX + B$, where Y is AWG,
m is the slope of Y versus X, the mil diameter,
and B is the y intercept of X on Y.

This assumes that the relationship between AWG and mil diameter is or nearly is a straight line. I've not plotted this to check it out. Otherwise, you'll have to use curve fitting techniques. I doubt that there is any derivable formula from first principals, i.e. a physical relationship between AWG and mil diameter—since AWG size is probably arbitrary. It would be interesting to see what the pioneers of American Wire did with this. Anybody know the history?]

Roy Osborne, Council Bluffs, Iowa. "Just received the new book, <u>Crystal Set Projects</u>. It is great, and as the introduction mentions, please do a Volume 2 taking off where Volume 1 ends (complex and innovative circuits). I was very impressed with the creativity of the Society members. The Krystal Kludge [project] demonstrates that scarcity of the old parts is no excuse to keep one from building working home brew radios. Thanks to all contributors for sharing your projects for all of us to enjoy building."

Robert St. John, Williamston, MI. "I believe that you are doing an excellent job with the Xtal Set Society newsletter. I look forward to each edition as it is published. I built crystal sets as a youngster and have only recently again become interested in building sets and collecting. I have a nice set of vintage Philmores, including some built in the 1920's. Altogether, I have 21 homebuilt and commercial sets."

Keith Erskine, internet. "I just had our cubscout den build the oatbox radio (plans on the Xtal website) with great success! The boys enjoyed wiring and soldering, but found winding the inductor a little challenging. One substitution we made was to use a 2-liter soda bottle in place of the oatmeal box. We still wound 40 turns of

24 AWG wire, but only put loops at every 10 winds instead of 5. Thanks for the plans!"

Allan Egleston, Sonora, CA. "I enjoyed the newsletter immensely. This month's experiment reminded me of an experiment that deForest did with an ordinary candle flame while developing the vacuum tube detector. Have any of you veterans heard of a Tesla coil being used for a receiving device? About 10 years ago, I heard a fellow say he and his company were using a Tesla coil for rx."

John Beegan, Streamwood, IL. John sent in some specs on coils he's been winding. "I now have 2 dozen coils wound, having used #18 gauge and #26 gauge wire. I used a peanut butter plastic jar, a plastic shampoo bottle, paper towel cores, a Kraft plastic parmesan cheese container, and oatmeal and salt boxes. Coil#14—Long plastic shampoo bottle resulted in 132 turns, calculated Henry 305; Coil#11—cardboard tube from a paper towel roll, varnished, 215 turns, calculated Henry 348; Coil#12—plastic peanut butter jar has 31 turns, calculated Henry 80.6; Coil#13—plastic Kraft parmesan cheese jar, 96 turns, calculated Henry 350. Coil #11 and #13 have very close values, but there is less wire in #13. I use toilet tissue cardboard cores and varnish them. Usually I varnish the coil, but have used Elmer's white glue (cheap) also carpenter's glue (titebond II) which I got at HomeDepot. Thanks for the fun!"

Ken Ladd, Minneapolis, MN. "I got the newsletter yesterday and have a comment regarding the resistance of a flame. This principle is used on my cousin's gas range. The ignition spark gap becomes filled with the flame when the burner ignites. The circuit then senses the spark gap resistance change and turns off the spark after a short time. He said he would have never figured it out if it were not for the manual. Kind of neat to see that some concepts never die." [Editor, A special thanks to Ken for sending in a bunch of old crystal set articles, we are putting them on our web page so everyone can share them. Thanks for your support Ken!]

Greg Constant, Austin, TX. "I was interested in Jerry Allen's article in the January issue because I have also tried to build 'full-wave' sets similar to Homer Davidson's design, and I also found that they did not produce added sensitivity. I haven't tried Jerry's set yet, but I thought I would pass along the two ideas I came up with. The goal of a 'full-wave' crystal set is to increase sensitivity by using both half cycles of the received RF signal in order to increase the received audio level. My idea, while not a true full-wave design, also makes use of both half cycles of the RF signal, but instead of feeding the results to one earphone as in most full-wave sets, I use two separate phones, one for each ear. Rather than attempting to increase the actual received audio volume, this approach helps to increase apparent sensitivity because you are now using both of your ears to listen to the signal. The advantage to this approach is that it can be used with almost any existing set design by adding D2, R2, and C2 to the typical detector circuit consisting of D1, R1 and C1. Another idea I use in conjunction with this is to use a pair of ear protectors to block out all background noise. I use a pair of large over-the-ear hearing protection devices like those used at a shooting range. I use one of the inexpensive models which can be obtained almost anywhere sporting goods are sold. I place them over both ears after inserting a crystal earphone into each ear. This works very well since virtually all background noise is eliminated leaving almost total silence which makes it much easier to hear a faint signal. [Editor, Greg is one of the winners of the recent crystal set projects contest.]

Dick Mackiewicz, Coventry, CT. "After reading the January 1997 issue of the newsletter, I have a few comments. Anyone building a new crystal set should consider including a switch to reverse the polarity of the detector diode/crystal. Often, amplitude modulation in not symmetrical. There are many reasons for this, including the manner in which the modulating audio is limited, component aging (especially in tube type transmitters), non-linearity of various components, etc. I'm sure others who have worked as broadcast engineers will confirm this. It is a definite advantage to be able to select the strongest sideband for detection. There is an easy way to accomplish full-wave detection in a crystal set. I prefer the term full-wave to push-pull, as push-pull really involves some phase inversion device inserted in the circuit to split the signal. I would suggest simply adding an extra wire to a pair of magnetic headphones and 'splitting' the phones so that each may be connected to the detectors for both sidebands. Note that this will not necessitate modification of the original tinsel cord. It may be necessary to reverse the wires on one receiver to "phase" the phones for maximum perceived volume. I realize that a typical 2000 ohm headset will now present a 1000 ohm lead to the tuned circuit, but this is not excessive. Many early crystal sets worked with telephone type receivers of 80 ohms. As this circuit requires only an extra diode and one extra wire, I would suggest people trying an A-B listening test; (A) series phones, one detector, (B) split phones, 180 degrees detectors. One simple way to make a set of magnetic phones more sensitive is to substitute thinner diaphragms for the originals. These may be cut from flat steel shim stock with a good sharp pair of scissors. Be sure to wear a pair of leather gloves when working with this stock as the edges can be very sharp! After cutting, use some fine emery cloth to eliminate these sharp edges. Let's say the original diaphragms measure .006-.007. Make new diaphragms of .005, .004, .003. The phones will overload sooner on strong signals but a suitable potentiometer in series with the phones will cure this problem. Remember to always slide diaphragms off phones rather than pulling them off."

VENDORS

Precision Scale Model Engineering
33 Harding Street, Milford, MA 01757-2215
508-478-3148—sent in by Dwayne Horton. They sell low-melt Bismuth alloy (woods metal) that Galena crystals should be potted in. They also sell various wires, screws, metal, and plastic. Send $4 for a catalog.

DC Electronics, P.O. Box 3203, Scottsdale, AZ 85271-3203, 1-800-467-7736

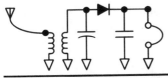

The Xtal Set Society Newsletter

Volume 7, No. 4   July 1, 1997

IN THIS ISSUE (#37) JULY 1, 1997

WWII UNDERGROUND XTAL RADIO
By Jim A. Penland

I have been told on good authority that during WWII the underground folks of Europe used crystal sets to listen to prohibited broadcasts. One of the sets utilized a loop wound around an inside door frame. The other

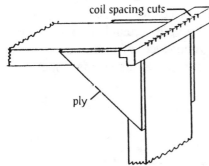

Figure 1: Door frame corner

components and earphone were installed within the door. To listen, the door (loop antenna) was opened to face the transmitting station, and thus maximize the signal, while holding the ear close to the hidden earphone installed in the door.

I duplicated such a set, shown in Figure 2, updated with a 1N34 diode. I made a wooden door-sized frame from scrap wood, measuring overall 36.75 inches by 80.75 inches and wound 11 turns around the frame. I used ¼ inch spacing (Fig. 1), starting and ending each turn on a terminal block with ¼ inch-spaced lugs (Photo 1). Using a simple classic circuit (Fig. 2) with a small 365 pF variable condenser, a 1N34 diode, a set of 2,000 ohm earphones, and a miniature 100 microamp meter to help with tuning, I readily received two local stations. The strongest was WNIS, with 50 kW on 850 kHz and located a distance of about 15 miles away. Its signal strength was about 35 microamps with the loop antenna alone. The loop set was very directional, as expected. I must have been a sight to the neighbors, walking around the yard with earphones on and carrying a door frame.

Photo 1: Close-up view of Jim's WWII loop radio.

I measured better than 400 microamps (with a different meter) when I attached a 150-foot antenna and a cold water pipe ground. I obtained the best results when both the antenna and ground were connected near the center of the coil. I used small alligator clips for all three taps to the terminal block.

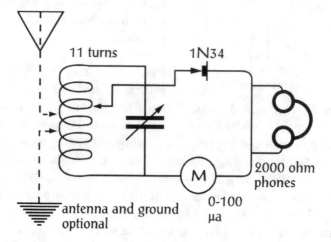

Figure 2: Schematic

[Editor. Thanks Jim for sending in this great project. It would be fun to hide one of these radios in a door and listen as they did during WWII. Below is a picture of Jim next to his creation.]

CAPACITANCE OF THE PARALLEL PLATE CAPACITOR
by Bill Simes

Physics books frequently derive the following general equation for calculating the capacity of a parallel plate capacitor in free space:

$$C = \frac{\varepsilon_0 A}{d}$$

where, C=capacitance in farads
A=plate area in square meters
d=plate spacing in meters
ε_0=permitivity of free space= 8.854 x 10^{-12} farads/meter.

Included with the equation is a caveat; for the equation to be accurate, either the plates must be closely spaced or d must be quite small relative to A. To me, this begs the question, what happens to the capacitance when the plate spacing increases? Rather than search literature for the answer, I chose the empirical route. That route required a suitable parallel-plate capacitor, a measuring method, and a modicum of data collection and analysis.

I cut two identical disks 5.128 inches in diameter from 1/8-inch aluminum stock. For the capacitor plates, the diameter was arbitrary. The ends of two plastic rods were accurately faced, center drilled and tapped 10-32. One rod was 3/4 inch in diameter, the other 1/2 inch, allowing it to fit in the jacobs chuck on the lathe tailstock. Center holes in the two disks were counter sunk. One-inch squares of 0.005-inch brass shim stock were punched in the center with a paper punch to make mounting holes without distorting the shim surface. These were mounted between the disks and the plastic rods to serve as connection terminals. After assembly, protrusions of the flat-head mounting screws were machined flush with the disk surface. The larger diameter rod was mounted in a 3-jaw chuck at the drive end of the lathe while the smaller was secured in the tailstock chuck. The tailstock moves laterally 1/10 inch per revolution of its turning wheel. I placed masking tape around the turning wheel, measured its diameter and marked the tape in increments of 1/10 of its circumference. These marks were then numbered 0 through 9 as the wheel turned counter clockwise (CCW). For an indicator, copper wire was duct taped to the lathe bed, and the free end was bent to align with the calibration marks. With the lathe chuck loose, I cranked the tailstock in a couple of inches, then backed off CCW to eliminate any play in the drive threads and to align the indicator wire with my zero marking. Finally, the disks were brought snugly together and the lathe chuck tightened to maintain this zero reference position. This completed the parallel plate capacitor needed for the experiment.

Since the numbers on most of my measuring instruments are in inches, I divided ε_0 by 39.37 inches/meter, making the general capacitance equation C=0.2249A/d pF/inch. The area, A, was then expressed in square inches and the spacing, d, in inches. The area of a 5.128-inch diameter disk is about 20.65 square inches. On making this substitution for A, the general equation for this particular capacitor becomes:

Cc=4.6447/d pF   Equation 1

Equation 1 will determine the calculated capacity values, designated Cc.

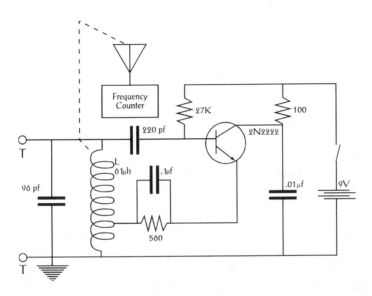

Figure 3: Hartley oscillator circuit used to measure capacity. Terminals TT connect to the capacitor being measured. The inductance L has 48 turns of #24 AWG closewound on a 1 ¼ inch diameter form. The coil is tapped 10 turns from the grounded end. Frequency is measured with a Mattco model 711 counter with its antenna in close proximity to the hot end of the coil.

For measuring capacitance, I chose the Hartley oscillator circuit shown in Figure 3; it was calibrated to determine the measured capacity values, designated Cm. For calibration standards, I used all the fixed capacitors I could find in my junk box that had capacities under 600pF and tolerances of no more than 2%. Recall that the condition for resonance in a LC circuit is that the magnitudes of the inductive and capacitive reactances be equal, i.e., $\omega L=1/(\omega C)$. Then $LC=1/\omega^2$, where L is inductance in henries, C is capacitance in farads and $\omega=2\pi f$, where f is frequency in hertz. To calibrate the oscillator for capacitance measurement, each "standard" capacitor was connected to the terminals, TT of Figure 3. The capacitance value shown on the capacitor was then recorded together with the oscillator frequency as indicated on the counter. From these data, ω was calculated and the reciprocal of ω^2 was plotted as a function of C. This is shown graphically in Fig. 4[1]. A linear regression[2] of the calibration data

113

yields an equation for the straight line that best fits the data. In this case that equation is:

$1/\omega^2 = 6.114E-5C + 5.8959E-15$.

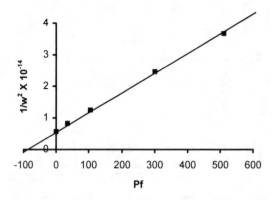

Figure 4: Graphical display of calibration data for measuring capacity with the circuit of Figure 3.

From this it is seen that the coefficient of C, which is the slope of the line, is 6.114E-5 Henries or 61.14μH. This then, is the inductance of the coil in the circuit of Fig. 3. If we let $1/\omega^2 = 0$, then C=-0.96418E-10 or -96.4pF. This would be the magnitude of the internal capacitance across the inductance in the circuit. The equation for the function becomes somewhat more manageable if ω is taken as 2π times the frequency in MHz instead of in Hertz and the capacitance is expressed in pF rather than farads. Then, on solving for C, the expression with its less cumbersome

exponents becomes: $C = \dfrac{(100/\omega^2) - 0.58959}{0.006114}$ Equation 2

With calibration complete, the capacitance at various plate spacings was found using Equation 2 and recorded as the measured capacity, Cm. Both Cm and Cc, the calculated capacity from Equation 1, are shown graphically in Figure 5 and again in tabular form in Table I. Notice in Figure 5 the steep rise in capacity as d approaches zero. No surprise here, since from Equation 1 it is seen that capacity goes to infinity as d approaches zero, yet in a space of only 0.02 inches the capacity plummets to less that 300pF. Because of the steep gradient, measurements in this region are inherently inaccurate. Fortunately, it doesn't matter because

114

this is also the region in which the general equation can be considered accurate.

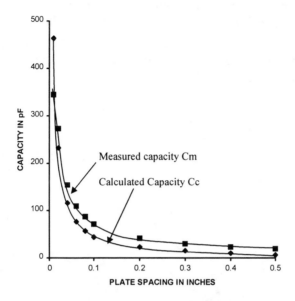

Figure 5: Measured capacity, Cm, and calculated capacity, Cc, plotted as a function of plate spacing.

Both Figure 6 and Table I show the ratios of measured to calculated capacitances for various values of d. The capacity as calculated from the general equation can be converted to its true value if multiplied by the correction factor, Cm/Cc. This correction factor is plotted as a function of d in Figure 6. A mathematical expression for the correction factor for this particular capacitor was found to be: $\left(1 + 1.7\sqrt{d}\right)$, where again, d is in inches. The plate spacing can be normalized by expressing it as the ratio of plate separation, d, to plate diameter, D, with both d and D measured in the same units of length. Spacing is then dimensionless and the correction factor expression becomes: $\left(1 + 3.8484\sqrt{d/D}\right)$.

This factor should apply to any parallel plate capacitor having circular plates. On examining these expressions one finds that as the plate separation approaches zero, the function approaches unity, the condition for which the text book equation is accurate. On the other hand, as the separation approaches ∞, Cc approaches zero. This makes their product indeterminate and the correction factor unnecessary as there is then no capacitance value to correct.

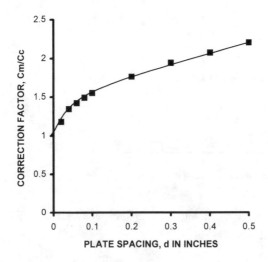

Figure 6: Ratio of Cm/Cc plotted as a function of plate spacing.

In conclusion, the data show that as the plate spacing of a parallel plate capacitor increases, its true capacity becomes greater than that calculated conventionally. Also, a mathematical expression for a correction factor was found allowing those capacity values to be quantified. In its dimensionless form the correction factor should apply to a parallel plate capacitor of any size so long as its plates are circular.

[1] (Incidentally, a graph of this type might have applications elsewhere. Since C was chosen as the independent variable, L must remain a constant independent of frequency, which makes L simply the slope of the linear plot. Also of possible interest is the negative capacity shown when the ordinate goes to zero. The magnitude of this negative capacitance is the sum of the internal stationary and distributed capacities that resonate with the coil.)

2 (Linear regression was calculated with Excel in Microsoft Office for Windows 95.)

Table 1: Measured capacity, Cm, and calculated capacity, Cc

d inches	f MHz	Cm pF	Cc pF	Cm /Cc	$1+1.7\sqrt{d}$	d/D	$1+3.84\sqrt{d/D}$
.01	.97xx	344	464.5	*	*	.0019	*
.02	1.0577	274	232.2	*	*	.0039	*
.04	1.2856	154	116.1	1.33	1.34	.0078	1.34
.06	1.4176	110	77.4	1.42	1.42	.0117	1.42
.08	1.5015	87	58	1.5	1.48	.0156	1.48
.1	1.5692	72	46.4	1.55	1.54	.0195	1.54
.2	1.7370	41	23.2	1.76	1.76	.0390	1.76
.3	1.8122	30	15.5	1.94	1.93	.0585	1.93
.4	1.8552	24	11.6	2.07	2.07	.0780	2.07
.5	1.8823	20.5	9.3	2.2	2.2	.0975	2.2

*area of uncertainty, see text

DETERMINING WIRE DIAMETER
By P.A. Kinzie

In the May 97 newsletter Bill McGraw asked the question, "Is there a formula to determine mil diameter from the AWG wire size?" Our editor, Phil, asked if anyone knew the history, and Phil A. Kinzie responded in depth.   Mr. Kinzie is also the author of "Crystal Radio: History, Fundamentals, and Design."

Phil writes, "The American Wire Gage as a name originated with the standardization of copper, aluminum, and certain resistance element wire sizes in the United States. It applies to a gage used earlier at the Brown and Sharpe Manufacturing Company, and which was later adopted by other manufacturers. It was known for many years as the B&S Gage, and is sometimes referenced by that name even today.

The B&S Gage was associated with a wire drawing process developed by J.R. Brown in 1857. This started with 0.46-inch diameter rod, which was drawn through a number of dies, decreasing the diameter step-by-step down to 0.005-inch diameter wire. Each die was (in theory) 0.8905258 times the diameter of the preceding size, and the series of wire sizes that resulted were stocked and sold by Brown and Sharpe.

Number 0000 (4/0) was assigned to the 0.46 inch rod, 000 (3/0) to the next smaller size, and on down to 0 gage, which was then followed by the familiar numbers still used today. After size 1, 35 more draws produced B&S Gage 36 with 0.005-inch diameter. The present wire tables extend to even finer wires, with the typical table ending at size 40 (0.003144-inch diameter). One table I have seen goes on up to AWG 50, which has a wire diameter of just under 1 mil.

A formula can be developed for calculating diameter in terms of AWG wire size, if we forget about the bigger rod sizes, that is, AWG numbers with more than one zero. Starting with AWG 0, which has a calculated diameter of 0.32486 inches, and remembering that AWG 1 is smaller in the ratio 0.8905258, then we can calculate:

AWG 0   = 0.32486 inches
AWG 1 (0.8905285) (0.32486)   = 0.2892962 inches
AWG 2 (0.8905285) (0.2892962)= 0.2576257 inches
And so on…

Of course this is not only tedious, but requires the use of multi-digit numbers throughout to maintain accuracy at the higher gage numbers. Fortunately, there are better ways.

Let c = 0.32486 (the constant for starting at AWG 0)
Let f = 0.8905258 (a fraction, which the ratio of any two successive wire
                diameters)

Then use the formulas below:

AWG Wire Diameter

0	c
1	cf
2	cf^2
3	cf^3

AWG "n" wire diameter = cf^n (where n is zero or greater). This can be written as an equation, $y = cf^x$ and in principle it can be plotted as y versus x on graph paper. This can be done directly from the wire tables instead of making lengthy calculations.

In practice, a plot of y versus x on ordinary graph paper over the full range of x is useless, because of the great change in y. The latter increases from about 3 mils (AWG 40) to over 0.3 inches (AWG 0). Even if just a portion of the table is plotted, covering often used sizes for coils, the resulting curve is not a straight line.

A more satisfactory plot results on logarithmic graph paper, where the values of both x and y coordinates are on logarithmic scales. The resulting plot is a straight line, and there is sufficient resolution for use in practical problems.

A still better approach for anyone with a scientific calculator is to use the exponential function, equivalent to f^x, multiplying the result by c, and reading the wire diameter for a given wire size as a result of a few key strokes. In fact, with a programmable calculator, a simple program can be stored to hold the entire range of AWG 0 through 50."

Short-Wave Crystal Radio Kit

The Society receives frequent requests for recommendations about good quality kits to buy and build. While investigating different kits we discovered that one of our own members, Mike Peebles, designs and provides the kits for Antique Electronic Supply. Mike has designed a number of kits for A.E.S., and we built the first one, #K-402, Short Wave Crystal Radio Kit. In the future, we plan to build the others and report to you.

The kit was neatly packaged. The parts included a 10-400pF variable capacitor, a 10-90pF trimmer capacitor, a 470pF disc capacitor, a 1N34 diode, coil form, wire, wood base, tuning knob and dial plate, and nuts and bolts; everything we needed was included. The radio took two evenings to put together (the average time might be 3-5 hours). You will need some tools, such as screwdrivers (Standard and Philips), wire cutters and strippers, a safety pin, a sharp knife, solder and solder iron, a drill with a 3/32 bit, scissors, pliers, craft glue, and a small file or sandpaper.

The directions were clear and easy to follow. When we got confused, it was easily cleared up by referring to the drawing of the set included in the instructions (Figure 10). The galvanized leads for the trimmer capacitor wouldn't take solder very well and needed to be sanded a bit before being soldered; this was the only problem we encountered building the set.

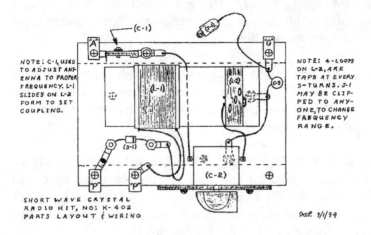

Figure 10: Short-wave crystal radio, parts layout and wiring

We had great fun listening to the set (of course)! We used a pair of 1910 Baldwin headphones, and a 75 foot horizontal antenna strung about 15 feet off the ground next to our building. We heard Radio Deutschabella (Germany?), the Christian Science Monitor, a Spanish speaking station (with references to Cuba and the Helms Burton law), Public Radio International, and many other stations we couldn't identify. We're located in the city, and there was considerable interference from local AM stations, so an antenna tuner or AM rejector trap would have been useful—Mike builds kits for each of these, and we will review them in upcoming issues of the Newsletter.

Mike builds the wooden base pieces in his workshop, where he also has built a great deal of children's furniture. We asked him how long he'd been building sets.

"I built my first set old out of the Cub Scout handbook when I was 10 years. It didn't work. I was frustrated, so I took it to this TV repair shop across the street to see if they could help me. I showed the man the book and my set. He switched a couple of wires around and said, 'you built it right but the diagram is wrong!' I told my den mother that the diagram was wrong, but she wouldn't believe me!"

Mike's favorite books as a kid were the Alfred P. Morgan's Boy's First Book of Radio and Electronics series. He went on to a career in electronics, and also worked as a purchasing and inventory specialist. He retired in 1987 and started back into he first radio interest, the crystal set.

[Editor's note 01/01/98: Mike's kit is now available from the Society. The part number is #K-402, and it sells for $24.95.]

MEMBERSHIP CORRESPONDENCE

[Editor.] Although we would like you to think we know everything, those of us at Society headquarters admit that we don't always know the answers to all the questions posed in this section of the newsletter. If you know the answer to a question, then please write in with your thoughts and ideas. If writing is too much trouble just call in your answer and leave us a message (make sure to leave your name or we will claim it was all our idea)! Many members have written asking what the heck happened to the bound version of Volume 6. We have decided to combine Volume 6 and 7 into a bound book, which should be available at the beginning of 1998.

Robert B. Foster, Greensboro, NC. "Sometime back I used to listen to the river pilots on the Mississippi and the Ohio on short-wave. I read that they were really reducing the transmission on short-wave. Do any of you ever listen to them and are there any frequencies anybody knows that they still use? Over here in North Carolina a lot of the stuff that used to be on short-wave like the Coast Guard and the rescue missions out of the Naval Base at Portsmouth have all but disappeared, too. I really enjoyed listening to the chatter on the rivers and got to know some of the folks by their voices. The new projects book is super!"

Charles J. Graham K6KDZ, Grass Valley, CA. "In regards to the continuing correspondence concerning the "foxhole radio," I have yet another variation of the same. Somewhere in the memory of my youth, it was explained that at the time this type of radio was being invented, there were not a wide variety of radio stations broadcasting. In fact, in wartime Europe, only a few select stations were on the air, thus the problem of selectivity was not a major one. In addition, finding components, especially coil wire, was a major problem.

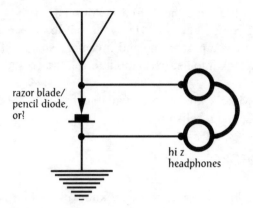

Figure 11: Charles Graham's "Simplest Radio"

Based on the above criteria, a reliable and simple fox hole radio could be built without a tuning device. It works well within the ground-wave area of a clear channel station. While a resident of Sacramento, I built such a radio and it actually would activate a speaker, a great idea for keeping small children occupied during the night. Clear channel KFBK, at 50,000 watts, was only a few miles away, so all conditions were at their best. 73's"

Joseph Cooper, Toronto, Canada "I want to offer your readers a supplemental sheet with an illustration for my recent article, The Directional Loop DX Xtal Set, which appeared in the new projects book. There is no charge for this, just provide a self-addressed stamped (US postage OK) envelope that can hold an 8½ by 11 sheet of paper. If members wish to correspond with me directly regarding the article and the illustration, they can use this address: 1575 Military Rd., Box 13-121, Niagara Falls, NY 14304. I check this box about once a month and would send responses immediately, but allow 6 weeks."

Marion McClure, Bloomington, IL. "I am looking for a schematic diagram that will use a tuning coil purchased from Antique Electronic Supply. It is called the 'Mascot' tuning coil from 1921. I would say it is a single coil with two sliders. Any suggestions on how to use this coil will be appreciated."

Jerry D. Bennett, Kennesaw, GA. "Has anyone experimented with a mechanical "Tikker" Detector in a xtal type set?" [Editor. In Volume 2, the March 1993 issue of the society newsletter is an article about the history of the Poulsen Tikker Detector. Also check out The Crystal Set Handbook pages, 41-49 where I built a modern day Tikker.]

Marc Ellis, Evanston, IL. [Editor. Marc found this great little gem in the March 1924 issue of Radio in the Home. The article is titled "Every Man His Own Variable Condenser." Thanks Marc!] "Radio fans here, although busily engaged in adding additional stages of radio frequency and audio amplification to their receiving sets as a result of the drop of nearly $2 in the retail price of tubes, have found time to chuckle heartily over the experiences, as published in a Minneapolis newspaper, of Paul Carroll, an electrician living at Excelsior, twelve miles west of the twin cities.

"Carroll, according to the story, built a one-tube set, expecting to use his bedspring for an aerial and a radiator pipe in his room for a ground. It wouldn't work. Dejectedly he sat on the edge of the bed, headphones over his ears. He heard music. Jubilant, he jumped to his feet. The music stopped. Now Carroll has evolved a system, somewhat strange, but the real thing, he insists. When he wants WGY he sits on the bed, with both feet off the floor. When he puts one foot on the floor he gets WOC; two feet on the floor he gets KDKA; lying on the bed, WJZ. To be technical about it, the human body is substituted for the condenser, Carroll says. Simple, isn't it?"

Lubos Rendek, internet. "Radio and electronics has been an interest of mine ever since one of my cousins assembled and demonstrated a crystal set to me one evening in a cold attic of a humble house in what was then known as Czechoslovakia. We lived on the eastern side of the 'Iron Curtain' and we were eager to glean any useful information about the free 'West'. The set would only pick up the strongest stations in the area, and these were actually only the regional services of Radio Prague via the re-broadcasting transmitter near Karlovy Vary. Nevertheless, my first experience with radio and with crystal sets in particular left a lasting impression on me. I would like to build a short-wave crystal set but haven't gotten around to it." [Editor. Lubos, we enjoyed your note. We just built a short-wave kit, it was great fun, and it is reviewed in this issue of the newsletter.]

Don Bullard, internet. "I am a radio amateur and I guess, like many others, one of the first things I ever built was a crystal set. I build one that was one of the projects with my '100 in 1 Knight Kit' when I was about 13 or so. I think there is a little bit of nostalgia at work here. There is still something magic about the most basic of radio receivers. But then, I'm not telling you anything new am I?"

XTAL FRIENDLY VENDORS

Amidon Associates PO Box 25867 Santa Ana, CA 92799 (714) 850-4660 call or write for catalog	ferrite rods
Antique Radio Classified P.O. Box 2 Carlisle, MA 01741 (508) 371-0512 call or write for free copy	monthly magazine for antique radio collectors, members report they love this monthly magazine, a must if you are into collecting
Lindsay Publications P.O. Box 538 Bradley, IL 60915-0538 (815) 935-5353	catalog of reprints and unusual technical books. Many of our members found us through Lindsay.
Midco, Dr. B.A. Turke P.O. Box 2288 Hollywood, FL 33022 (954) 925-3670 send $2 for catalog	variety of crystal set parts You can't always reach Dr. Turke on the phone but you will get a catalog if you send the $2.
Monitoring Times Grove Enterprises P.O. Box 98 Brasstown, NC 28902 (800) 438-8155	magazine for short-wave radio and scanning enthusiasts. Many members have found us through MT's favorable reviews of our books. MT is very supportive to the antique radio community. If you are interested in scanning and sw, this is the magazine.
Mouser Electronics 1-800-346-9873	crystal earphones, diodes, and other electronic parts
The Xtal Set Society 1-800-927-1771	365pf variable caps, crystal earplugs, and more soon.

MORE NEWSLETTER ARTICLES!

As you may have noticed this issue has a few more articles than usual. After including more construction projects in the last few issues the response has been positive. Please continue to send in good quality projects, reviews, and questions & answers. **The more you send in, the more we'll print!** We will print projects, book and kit reviews, and theoretical articles. The Society newsletter is now completely driven by the members, and this is terrific! The newsletter will continue to be 6 pages long, with a few "bonus" issues like this one. Please feel free to call Rebecca at (314) 725-1172 if you have any questions about submitting an article.

XTAL SET SOCIETY WEB PAGE

The Society web page now includes the MidnightScience Bookstore. This on-line store has color photographs of all the books we carry and includes complete descriptions. You can order books by e-mail if you wish. If you have purchased from the Society using Visa or MC in the last year, we have your information on file and you can simply send an e-mail to **xtalset@midnightscience.com** to order. Please give your return e-mail address or phone number so we can reach you if we have a question. Our site address is: **www.midnightscience.com**

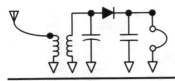

The Xtal Set Society Newsletter

Volume 7, No. 5   September 1, 1997

In This Issue (#38) September 1, 1997

A Capacitive Transducer Receiver
By William Simes

When first introduced to electrostatics, we learn that like charges repel while unlike charges attract. This being the case, it follows that when a dc voltage is applied to a parallel plate capacitor, one plate becomes charged positively and the other is charged negatively. Then according to Coulomb's law, there must be a force tending to pull the two plates together. If the polarity of the applied voltage is reversed, a force of equal magnitude still tends to pull the plates together. For a given capacity then, the force of attraction between the plates might reasonably be expected to be a function only of voltage magnitude completely independent of the polarity.

Now suppose the charging voltage source is alternating, moreover, it is alternating at radio frequency. If the amplitude of this voltage remains constant, the mechanical inertia of the metal plates might well integrate the rapidly changing force into a steady state force. What would happen then if instead of maintaining a constant amplitude, the amplitude of this applied RF voltage were modulated at an audio rate? Would not the

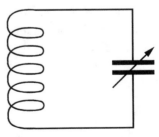

Figure 1: Circuit of the capacitive transducer

Photo 1: Bill's capacitive transducer

Plates attract one another (move toward and away from each other) at the modulated audio rate? What if now, one plate were stationary with a relatively high mass while the other was merely a thin conductive diaphragm of relatively low density? Would not such an arrangement serve as a sound transducer for the modulating audio? These are questions that come to mind. If the reasoning is sound (no pun intended) it should be possible to devise a variable capacitive transducer allowing the entire AM wave train to be received without using a rectifying detector that discards half of the received signal to recover the modulating information. In pursuit of the theory, I assumed some physical dimensions within the whittling capabilities of my shop and did some cursory arithmetic. The results weren't promising, but I built an experimental model anyway. The completed circuit for an AM receiver using the capacitive transducer is shown in Fig. 1. Circuit wise, this may well be the simplest receiver yet! A functional diagram of the transducer is shown in Fig. 2.

Thinking it would be less embarrassing if there were no witnesses to an experiment with probable failure, I loaded the transducer, a loop antenna and a portable picnic table in the car and set out alone to test my theory. I parked the car to the side of a lightly traveled road near a local broadcast station antenna. At a distance about equal to the radius of the tower guy wire anchors, I set up shop and slowly tuned the transducer. Much to my surprise the signal was there! Fidelity was good and clear. Tuning, however, was critical, so critical in fact that thermal distortions from the hot sun made it necessary to retune frequently.

Photo 2: Testing the transducer
behind the local AM station.

Elated with the test results, I packed up, drove home, and returned with my wife, Elaine, and a camera to repeat the experiment; this time I had a witness and a means to photographically document the event. The good news from this exercise is that the device functions as planned, responding faithfully to both positive and negative excursions of the modulated carrier while using neither a rectifying detector nor conventional headphones. Circuit-wise it's hard to imagine a simpler receiver. The bad news is that you have to be close to the broadcast tower to receive the signal. From home, 3 miles from the tower, I heard nothing. I didn't try it at distances in between. Clearly, the device is not yet a DX machine and there is room for much improvement. I tried replacing the Reynolds wrap aluminum diaphragm with metalized Monokote. It's a heat-shrink plastic film for covering model airplanes. It creates a beautiful, mirror-like diaphragm. It works as a tuning capacitor, as evidenced by strong reception when I hooked up a diode and phones. As a transducer, however, it was a complete bust, so, it's back to Reynolds Wrap.

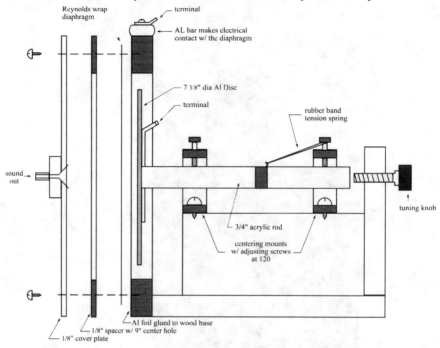

Figure 2: Functional diagram of the capacitive transducer.

GRID LEAK DETECTOR ONE TUBE RADIO
By John M. Franke, WA4WDL

As you suggested in several issues of your publication, perhaps it is time to expand the coverage to include simple vacuum tube radios. Having an aversion to regenerative receivers, I decided to try a simple grid leak detector. Besides, grid leak detectors predate regenerative and superregenerative detectors. I chose a 1G4 GT/G triode for several reasons. First, I have a half dozen of them. Second, they have a directly heated cathode requiring only 50 milliamps at 1.4 volts filament power. Almost any triode could be used. But, in keeping with the spirit of antique radio, directly heated cathodes should be preferred. Several suggested tubes would be the old 5 volt '01A and for 2 volt filaments, a type 30 or a type 1H4. Don't overlook the use of 7 pin, miniature 1.5 volt tubes formerly used for portable battery powered radios. Ideally, a tube having a low amplification factor but high transconductance is most desirable.

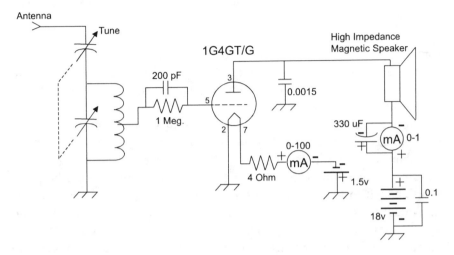

Figure 2: Functional diagram of the capacitive transducer.

Whatever tube you select, make sure you can find a socket for it. Sockets are becoming almost as hard to find as are the vacuum tubes to go in them. This is especially true for the large odd sockets needed for transmitting tubes. Fortunately, the 1G4 GT/G uses a common octal socket. I prefer molded sockets over phenolic wafer sockets because of their superior durability. Ceramic sockets are the most appealing but hardest to find. I was lucky and found a special relay socket that has an octal socket and eight screw terminals all molded together in one piece. The screw terminals permit changes to be easily made. I do not even have to turn the socket over to get at each pin. It is ideal for bread boarding low frequency vacuum tube circuits.

For my first attempt at using a grid leak detector, I decided to use the same center tapped-tuned circuit that I used to test crystal detectors. The complete schematic is shown in Figure 3. The tuning capacitor is a dual section 25-620 micromicrofarad variable. The coil is a surplus tapped air core coil that happens to tune the A.M. broadcast band. A second set up was tried with a link coupled input-tuned circuit. Since I use a high

131

impedance antique magnetic speaker with the crystal sets, I used the same speaker as a load for the grid leak detector. Performance improvement or lack thereof can be determined by measuring the a.c. audio signal across the speaker winding. I did try an output transformer and regular 8 ohm dynamic speaker, which is not as efficient as the old magnetic speaker but nevertheless quite usable. Headphones were unbelievably loud for local stations!

Having selected a tube, or valve, and a tuned circuit, the next item to be considered is the grid leak network. The grid resistor should be as high in value as practical. The greater the resistance, the greater the receiver sensitivity. The upper limit is determined by the vacuum tube internal and external leakage current and by blocking from strong signals (not a real problem at my location.) A good compromise is between 0.5 and 3 megohms. The product of the grid leak resistance and the grid leak capacitance determines the detector time constant which should be made short enough to follow speech or music but long enough to filter out the individual radio frequency cycles. This is the same design criteria found with crystal or any other type detectors. The product of the resistance in megohms and the capacitance in micromicrofarads should not exceed 200 according to reference 1, page 100. So, I use a 1 megohm resistor shunted with a 200 micromicrofarad (200 picofarads to you younger folks) capacitor. I have a few old Sprague transmitting type mica capacitors with screw terminals that look great next to the glass vacuum tube and have very low leakage. The grid leak resistor is conveniently mounted with solder lugs on the capacitor. I tried a 100 micromicrofarad disc ceramic capacitor in parallel with a 2 megohm grid leak resistor this did reduce the plate current somewhat but did not seem to affect the sensitivity.

Next, the actual wiring commences. Note that the positive side of the filament is connected to common. Reference 1, page 98 states "The detecting of the average tube is about twice as good when using the positive terminal as the common junction...this improvement being due to the shape of the grid-current potential curve." If the circuit common is connected to the negative side of the filament, the other end of the filament is now 1.4 volts positive with respect to the grid and is at or near cutoff. Van Der Bijl, page 335 in reference 5, states it clearer, "In order to secure the best results with this type of circuit it is necessary to operate on that part of the grid voltage, grid current characteristic which shows the greatest curvature, and simultaneously adjust the plate potential to such a value that the operating point on the plate current, grid potential characteristic lies in the region where this characteristic (transconductance) is steepest. This usually requires that the grid be maintained at a positive potential with respect to the negative end of the filament. The simplest way to secure this is to connect the grid circuit to the positive end of the filament...instead of to the negative end as is commonly done in other circuits. This makes the filament negative with respect to the grid, the average potential difference between them being in the neighborhood of the value where the grid current characteristic has its greatest curvature." In practice, I found the factor of two for the sensitivity to be very accurate. It did not matter which filament pin was positive, but the circuit common had to be connected to whichever pin was connected to the positive terminal of the A battery. I use a 0.1 microfarad transmitting-type mica capacitor to bypass the plate supply and one rated at 0.0015 microfarad to bypass the plate to ground.

As previously noted, the 1G4 GT/G tube requires .05 amp at 1.4 volts for filament power. A fresh standard dry cell puts slightly more than 1.55 volts. To extend the tube life, I use a 4 ohm resistor in series with the filament, dropping the filament voltage just a tad. With a fresh battery, the filament current is 46 milliamps. There was no discernible difference in operation. The resistor also reduces the inrush of current that occurs before the filament reaches operating temperature. Because the filament/cathode is directly heated, warm up time is only about one second. The filament voltage can be below the rated value in this application because the plate current is below the typical operational value of 2.3 milliamps and saturation is not a problem. Maximum plate current is dependent on filament temperature and space charge effect. I included a 100 milliammeter in the filament circuit for checking the filament battery condition and just because I like meters.

Even if the tube is operated at rated filament voltage, do not expect the tube to give off a bright glow. The filament power is only 70 milliwatts. However, a faint glow is visible with the receiver on in a darkened room. The old '01A tubes consumed 0.25 amps at 5 volts or 1.25 watts. Most receiving tubes consumed 0.3 amps at 6.3 volts or about 1.9 watts! Unlike most tubes, the 1G4 GT/G remains cool even after hours of operation. The brighter the filament, the shorter the tube and battery life. Those No. 6 dry cells are expensive and hard to find. But, at this low current, standard D cells work just fine and are more compact. Almost makes you want to try transistors—almost!

One nice thing about grid leak detectors is the inverse dependence of plate current on signal strength. The stronger the signal, the lower the plate or anode current. Hence, you do not have to worry about pegging the meter on strong signals. I use a 0-1 milliammeter in the plate circuit to monitor the circuit operation and provide a simple tuning indicator and besides, it looks spiffy. The meter is shunted with a 330 microfarad capacitor to damp its motion somewhat and bypass it for audio frequencies. Mounting the meter upside down, the motion of the needle is more akin to a normal signal strength meter, i.e. an increasing signal causes the meter to swing to the right. But, I like my meters right side up, and it does not take long to get used to dipping the plate current. The same meter could be used, with a switch and multiplier and/or shunt resistors, to monitor or check the condition of the A and B batteries or filament current.

Smith, reference 3, recommends a B supply or plate voltage slightly greater than the filament voltage times the amplification factor of the tube. For the 1G4 GT/G, this would mean a plate supply somewhat above 12.4 volts. Plus, you must account for the voltage drop in the load. In my case, the load is a magnetic speaker with a d.c. resistance of 1225 ohms. In Smith's application, a field-strength meter, the load was a 0-1 milliammeter, typically about 50 ohms. He used a triode connected 1T4-GT miniature vacuum tube and a plate supply up to 22.5 volts. In a prior article, reference 4, he used a type 19 or 1J6 with both triode sections tied in parallel and a plate supply up to 52.5 volts. But, the need for a plate supply that large was to assure linear operation for both weak and strong signals. For just weak signals, a lower voltage is acceptable. However, I found the volume to be a direct function of the plate voltage. This is to be expected because the transconductance of the tube is strongly dependent on plate current, particularly for low values of plate current. The main reason for the rapid increase in transconductance is the steep drop in plate resistance as the plate current rises. The amplification factor stays relatively constant and the transconductance is simply the amplification factor divided by the plate resistance. The final value selected for the plate supply was 18 volts because it is easily obtainable from two common 9 volt transistor radio batteries and the no signal plate current is under 1 milliamp.

According to page 231 in reference 2, the grid leak detector radio should be about ten times as sensitive as the crystal detector, due to the gain of the vacuum tube. Also, the tube does not load the tuned circuit as much as a crystal detector. Therefore, for the same tuned circuit tap position or antenna coupling, the grid leak detector is more selective. Or, for a given selectivity, the tap position can be moved closer to the antenna connection or the antenna coupling can be increased, resulting in louder volume. The antenna coupling would be an excellent way to control volume. My next grid leak detector receiver will have a variable coupler as part of the input tuned circuit to function as a volume control.

As an indication of sensitivity improvement over a crystal receiver, the MRL tuned circuit was connected to a modulated radio frequency generator tuned to 1 MHz and the generator output adjusted to produce a crystal (1N270) current of 30 microamps. The audio signal across the speaker winding was 50 millivolts rms. The same tuned circuit was connected to the 1G4 GT/G and the plate current, with an 18 volt plate supply, dropped from a no signal value of 0.64 milliamps to 0.30 milliamps. The audio signal signal across the speaker winding was now 170 millivolts rms, an increase or voltage gain of 3.4 or a power gain of 11.56.

What next? The next experiment will be to try a pentode or tetrode form of grid leak detector. Then perhaps a comparison between a grid leak detector and a crystal detector followed by a vacuum tube audio amplifier.

References:

1. Hausmann, Erich; Goldsmith, Alfred N.; Hazeltine, Louis A.; Hogan, John V. L.; Morecroft, John H.; Canavaciol, Frank E.; Gibson, Robert D.; and Hoernel, Paul C.: Radio Phone Receiving, D. Van Nostrand Company, New York, 1922.

2. Morecroft, John H.: Elements of Radio Communications, John Wiley & Sons, Inc., New York, 1934.

3. Smith, W. W.: "A Grid Leak Type Field-Strength Meter," Radio, February 1942, pp. 32, 33, and 61.

4. Smith, W. W.: "A Highly Sensitive Field Strength Meter," Radio, March 1940, pp. 37-39 and 74-77.

5. Van Der Bijl, H. J.: The Thermionic Vacuum Tube, McGraw-Hill Book Company, Inc., New York, 1920.

How to Make a Double Crystal Receiver

One of our members, Dr. E.E. Taylor, sent us a copy of this article some time ago. We just found it in the Xtal vault and thought everyone might enjoy it. It was published in a book called Radio Receivers, by Radio Digest in 1924. The subtitle says, "Use of Two Crystals in Set Helps Increase the Volume."

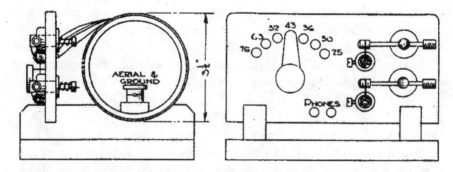

Figure 4: The figure notes read, "Each crystal detector consists of a central pivot drawn in by a spring, a cat-whisker stem slidable through a transverse hole in the end of the pivot, and a ring or washer of insulation material surrounding the pivot and having a transverse slot for the cat-whisker stem to rest in."

Here is an excerpt from the article. "In the set shown in the illustrations, I have designated the dimensions and number of turns which have been found most satisfactory. The construction, as shown, is easy to build, and many of the details are left to the ingenuity of the builder, but one hint must be given, and that is, to solder the wires to the switch point before the coil is secured to the base, as otherwise it will be difficult to get the soldering iron in between the coil and the panel."

The author, whose name is never given, goes on to say that two crystals are better than one, if they are in reverse order in the circuit. "Since a crystal acts only as a rectifier, each crystal can use only one-half of the wave. Now, if the conductivity of the crystal in the other direction would be absolutely zero, then the energy from the other half of the wave would merely be sent back into the oscillatory circuit to add to the energy of the next wave. But actually the conductivity of a crystal is not absolutely zero in either direction. It is merely greater in one direction than in the other. If, now, another crystal could utilize that half of the wave which the first crystal cannot use, then substantially all the energy of the waves would either be rectified to audio frequency or returned to the oscillatory circuit."

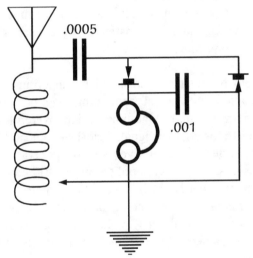

Figure 5: Double Crystal Receiver schematic

Figure 5 shows the schematic of the double crystal receiver. The author says if you can tinker until you get the adjustments just right, you should hear a louder signal than if you used just one detector. List of parts includes 2 detectors, a 4x9 panel, a .0005 mfd capacitor, a .001 mfd capacitor, coil wire, switch arm and taps, and binding posts. The cost in 1924 was $5.10!

Unified Theory of One-Tubers

By Phil Anderson, WØXI, Lawrence, KS

What's a "One-Tuber?" A one-tuber is slang for a radio consisting of just one tube. Such radios appeared in the late 1920's along with the crystal set.

Why did radio buffs build radios with just one tube? First of all, they were seeking better sensitivity; they wanted to copy the weaker stations too. Second, better selectivity was possible if more gain (better sensitivity) were built into a set. Finally, while multi-tube sets provided even better performance, tubes and batteries were expensive, so many designed and/or built one-tubers.

Signals too weak to be detected and heard by an optimized crystal set could often be copied with a set containing one or more tubes (or transistors for modern designs). One-tube designs were classified by the way in which they boosted the signal: grid-leak detector, tuned radio frequency (TRF), reflex, regenerative, super-regenerative, and audio boosted. In all designs, the power supplied by the "B" battery is used, in part, to boost the signal; that is, the battery, tube, and circuitry combine to add power to the signal so that it could be heard. "B" voltage ranged, depending upon design, from about 12 volts to as high as 50 volts. A low voltage "A" battery was needed too—typically about 1.5 volts—to supply power to the tube filament.

Grid-leak detectors and tuned radio frequency sets boosted signal power by increasing the effective current provided to the phones. Reflex radios boosted the radio frequency of the signal—often using a separate crystal detector too—and then rerouted the derived audio signal back through the same tube to boost it hence the name reflexive.

The regenerative and super-regeneratives were fundamentally different, not boosting the signal one time (through the tube) but many times over. These sets used feedback techniques for the first time in radio circuitry. The output (at the radio reception frequency) was fed back (looped back) to the input of the set over and over again, boosting the signal greatly.

All of these methods resulted in improvements in sensitivity and selectively, and each set had its own characteristics. We'll review these designs and provide examples and plans in future issues.

MEMBERSHIP CORRESPONDENCE

David Simpson, Laurel, Maryland. "Some years ago I enjoyed DXing on the AM broadcast band. My favorite reference book was the "North American Radio-TV Station Guide" by Vane A. Jones (now out of date and out of print). It listed all the broadcast AM, FM, and TV stations in North America by location and frequency, and included some other information, such as the station's transmitter power. Does anyone know if there is a similar reference available today that lists all the AM broadcast stations in the United States?"

Peter Mennell, Atlanta, Georgia. "I'm 53 and I remember to this day building, and listening to, my various Xtal Radios as a boy in Germany. The factory built crystal radio in the early 50s in Germany was the WISI model, with plug-in cat whiskers 'detector.' Do you know anything about it? It was red in color, with some blue, and about the size of a large soap box. (Of course soap boxes were the cabinet of choice of a lot of projects in those days.)

"I've been trying for years to locate articles in late 50s U.S. electronics magazines written by Art Trauffer (believe spelling is correct). I still lived in Germany at the time and was never able to build any of his transistor projects because I couldn't get the specified parts, and didn't know how to substitute. I remember one of his projects involved basically a crystal radio, using wire wound around a fairly large cabinet for an antenna, with a 1 or 2 transistor amplifier added, and, of course, headset reception. I would really appreciate any help in locating Art Trauffer's articles."

Peter Berrett VK3KAT, internet. "I was searching on the Internet and came across your site. I have some ideas for crystal sets. I'd be interested to know if any of these have ever been done before. a) A stereo FM crystal set (I believe it can be done). b) An 80m band crystal set QRP transmitter. Yes, that's right, transmitter. My theory goes something like this. One could make a small oscillator and use a small amount of current to power it. The current could be supplied as follows. One or two simple coil and capacitor combinations are tuned to broadcast strong AM stations. Instead of decoding the tuned signals, the alternating current would be rectified by the use of diodes to form pulsating DC current. Since most of the current would come from the carrier of the AM station, the pulsating DC current would have some degree of consistency. This could be smoothed out by the use of capacitors. Having established a low power source, this power could be used to drive a small 80m transmitter (CW). I don't know how much power a crystal set can generate, but I know that QRP hams have sent messages around the world on flea power. The same principle could be used to power a FM stereo crystal set. What do your members think?"

Ian Aldridge, Sydney, Australia. "As a boy not only were crystal radios a fascination, but also Meccano. Unfortunately my parents bought the Meccano for my brother and I had to sneak into his room to play with it. Now years later, Meccano was a distant memory, then you added the vintage crystal radio article section to your Webpage. I was ecstatic. A crystal set made with Meccano! All my Christmases had come at once. I took the challenge to replicate it. I started by scaling the components from the picture by using known Meccano parts and fabricated the more expensive or unavailable components. The two spider web coils were 4 inches diameter, on which, I wound ninety turns of 25 AWG gauge wire to give 375 microhenries inductance. The variable capacitor with 1.8mm spacing between the plates (2.7mm or three washers between plates of same potential) gave 25 to 210 picofarads capacitance. I must admit that I fluked these values and landed close to the broadcast band (567kHz-16440kHz calculated). I was also lucky to have a cats whisker assembly that fitted perfectly into the Meccano single bent strip. I wired one spider web as an untuned antenna coil and am able to vary the coupling with the tuned circuit to provide good selectivity and sensitivity. I took the replica to my local Historical Radio Society meeting and the members were impressed, even more so when I showed them your article. I thank you and your contributing member for this gem of information and I now have an amazing piece of history in my collection. Keep up the good work!"

Jim Clark, Mesa, AZ. "I am honored and thrilled that you elected to use the photo of my Matchbox Crystal Radio for the cover of the new book. I must say that I am very impressed with the quality of projects that it contains. It is obvious that there is a considerable wealth of talent among the Society membership. Well done, everybody!"

Kevin Norton, Randolph, MA. "A quickie experiment for the bulletin.... Simply attach a long antenna in series with a hi Z earphone and ground. The 'slinky' sounding chirps or pings (among the 60hz) are worldwide ELF natural static crashes from strong lightning activity." [Editor. Kevin would like to correspond with someone, 20 Julian Rd., Randolph, MA 02368.]

Photo #3: Philmore American Explorer VC-2000, p.16 of Toy Crystal Radios, by permission of Eric Wrobbel. See vendors section for more.

David Shaw, England. "I am a teacher of special needs working with disaffected teenagers in Manchester in the north of England. One of my 'party tricks' to get these youngsters re-motivated to learn and to build their self-esteem, is to build little electronic projects with them. I am a radio ham, so crystal sets are always a good starting point. It is always rewarding to see their faces when they can listen to their favorite music station for free on a crystal radio."

Gilbert Hofacker, internet. "For the fellow who was asking about shipping utilities on shortwave in the last issue...computer packet has replaced morse code, and most voice is done in ssb. He should check out the 157-169 maritime band if he has a scanner. Also check out the Mississippi radio net on the 200 mHz band, most of the system is set up like a cellular telephone system."

Vic Spicer, Winnipeg, Manitoba. "The July issue was great! Charles Graham's 'Simplest Radio' indeed works. I used a piece of fused silicon as a detector, and I get a mix of out two strong AM stations at 680 and 1210 kHz. You can sort of train your brain to filter out the station you don't want. The AES kit you reviewed looks really nice. I've never had much luck making SW xtal sets work in my location. The signals are there, I just need over 20 db of audio gain to fish them out! Anyone have any suggestions on this? Maybe a one-tube regenerative set is what I need?"

Allan Egleston, Sonora, CA. Allan has been building a foxhole set from a book called, "All about Radio and Television" by Jack Gould. It was published in 1958 by Random House. It has plans for a fox-hole set on page 61, so check your local library if you are interested. He also says, "continuing on boat frequencies, Mr. Foster should check out Radio Shacks marine R/F frequency quide."

John O'hara, Bridgewater, NV. "Since joining the Society, I have built three crystal sets. It has been fun, fun, and fun. If the society should ever name any of us for the best idea of the year, I would nominate Greg Constant of Austin, TX. His suggestion was to use hearing protection ear muffs in order to reduce background noise (Vol. 7 No. 3, Issue #36). I tried it, and it made the too faint to copy signals readable! After putting on the muffs, I could actually understand the speech. Thank you Greg."

Richard Spratley, Chesapeake, VA. "I received my most welcome issue today of the "XSS" newsletter, Volume 7, No. 4. I was delighted to see the plans of "A Crystal Set for the Boy Builder." This is to advise that I had built that set from those same plans [some time ago I am 72 now), and it turned out very nicely, it is a very good performing set. I am enclosing a photo of my set so that everyone can see what the set will look like when built according to the plans by Mr. Will H. Bates."

Photo# 4: Richard's crystal set, built from the "Boy Builder" plans

VENDORS

We found a neat little booklet for those of you interested in seeing color pictures of toy crystal radios. Toy Crystal Radios is published by Eric Wrobbel. It is a 26 page full-color booklet, 6 x 9. At first glance it didn't look like much, but when we opened it up, we were surprised by the beautiful pictures and artistic layout. Eric has captions, written in his own cartoon-style printing, under all of the over 50 radios pictured. The photographs are of great quality. Some of these radios have been mentioned by members in the past: the Rocket Radios, Spy "Pen" radios, and Pocket radios. The booklet is expensive—$19.95 including shipping—but well worth it if you are interested in these photos. Eric explained that he produces these in very small numbers, and with the full color photos the price to print them is very high. He gave us permission to reprint one of the photographs, of course the black and white doesn't do it justice, but you can get the idea, see page 7. If you are interested in obtaining one of these booklets, send a check or money order to Eric Wrobbel, 20802 Exhibit Court, Woodland Hills, CA 91367. Eric also has some black and white photo booklets about transistor radios ranging from $7 to $10, if you would like to talk to him about those you can reach him at (818) 884-2282. Tell him the Xtal Set Society sent you!

We met the owner of Play Things of Past, Gary Schneider, at the Elgin, Illinois antique radio meet. In the past we had listed his address but not given much information. The catalog is 88 pages long and is divided into 6 areas: transformers, tubes, parts, literature, books, and magazines. He has a huge selection of variable condensers, coils, sockets, and much more. If you want a copy of his catalog, send $6 to Gary Schneider, Play Things of Past, 9511-23 Sunrise Blvd. Cleveland, OH 44133. Gary explained that he does not make money on the catalog, he asks for $6 to cover just the printing and postage for it. He also has a retail store at 3552 West 105th St. in Cleveland.

Another Radio Building Contest

Our new projects book has been very well received, if you missed the review of our book in the August issue of QST, please pick up a copy or visit our website. This means, of course, that we should get started on another. We would like your input and ideas as we are in the planning and development process. Along with more complicated crystal set projects, we would also like to include a few of each of the following: grid-leak, TRF, reflex, regenerative, and super-regenerative sets. Again, we will have to include 3 or so basic projects at the front for the beginner, but that doesn't mean we can't include more complicated sets in the rest of the book. How can you increase your chances of winning? Include detailed, step-by-step directions with plenty of drawings and a photograph of the finished product. A few members actually shipped us the radio they built for the last contest, which really drew attention to their project. The project deadline has not been set yet, but it should be in the Spring. The prize will be $50 and 5 copies of the book for each winning article, and you may submit as many articles as you like.

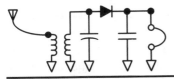

The Xtal Set Society Newsletter

| Volume 7, No. 6 | November 1, 1997 |

IN THIS ISSUE (#39) NOVEMBER 1, 1997

THE "CIGAR BOX" CRYSTAL RADIO SET
By Joseph Cooper - VE3FMQ

The revival of the practice of smoking Cigars helps to bring back a novel crystal radio set from the 1950's.

This article will show the reader how to build a crystal radio set using a Cigar box in a novel way. The plans that are presented here are based upon a design that was found in a Radio/TV magazine from the early 1950's. This original design has been updated with modern parts that are easy to locate.

The set has good selectivity and sensitivity characteristics, partly because the tuning coil doubles as a loop antenna. When properly employed, this type of antenna tends to be "quieter" than long wires types, while at the same time having high gain. A further benefit of using a loop is that it is directional, which allows the set to be "aimed" at a station in order to pick up the strongest signal, or turned away from sources of radio noise.

One notable feature of the design is its ease of construction, which makes this project a good "first crystal set." As it requires only the simplest of tools and a minimum of supervision, it is suitable for an older child or young teen, though even the more experienced builder will still enjoy putting one together. You will find the performance level is equal to a regular coil design. A striking benefit of using a loop for an antenna is the elimination of the need for a ground connection, with the result being that the set is fully portable.

To hear more distant signals, an external antenna can be attached using the connector provided for greater sensitivity. Once this is done, the loop antenna becomes an isolated L/C circuit that operates only as a tuning coil. If you wish to experiment with the design, taps can be added to the loop for greater selectivity in specific portions of the broadcast band. These taps also allow the set to be tuned to the lower shortwave frequencies as well, where foreign broadcasters can be heard. The efficiency of the small loop is surprising, and the design presented is quite useful for listening to local stations with only a headset. To hear more distant stations you also may use an audio amplifier.

A very earnest young man uses a cigar box radio that he built himself. Picture taken in the early 1950's.

The loop antenna is also useful in environments with high levels of electrical noise (such as apartments or downtown areas), as it is "quieter" than the long wire type. This "quiet" characteristic is due to the loop being more sensitive to the magnetic component of the received radio

146

wave, which emphasizes the information portion of the signal. This is the opposite of the long wire antenna. The long wire tends to be more sensitive to the voltage component, which carries more electrical noise and static with the information. (The bibliography at the end of this article will suggest more readings on this topic to help explain why this is so).

The loop antenna's main virtue, however, is its ability to be highly directional. One is able to improve the reception of a broadcaster by simply pointing the receiving side of the loop in the direction of their transmitting antenna. You can also separate out the skywave component of the signal (the part that bounces off of the ionosphere and returns to the earth) from the groundwave component (the signal that comes directly from the transmitting antenna) by tilting the box to a 45 degree angle. The small size of the set easily allows for this type of experimenting.

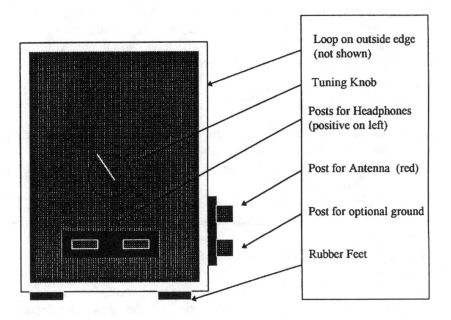

Figure 1: Front of Crystal Radio Set

Part of the attraction of this project is the cigar box itself. For many it may provide an extra bit of nostalgia when undertaking the project. You may remember having used these boxes to store treasured items back in the time of your youth (and possibly for many years past that point as well). Due to their durability and attraction, many old cigar boxes are found today in antique and collectable stores, but because of the resurgence of cigar smoking, it is not as difficult as it once was to find a supply of used cigar boxes.

If you don't know anyone who smokes cigars, then inquire at a store that sells them. They often have empty boxes from their sales of single cigars. These boxes should be made of either strong cardboard or paper covered wood, and should sell for no more than $1 or $2 (some specialty wooden boxes will be more expensive, but these are not required for this design). Obtain a large sized box that holds two rows of cigars (approx 5½" x 9" x 2½"), not the smaller box that holds only one row. The small boxes that are used for European and specialty cigars will not provide the space and size needed for this project.

Finally, we sincerely ask the reader not resort to smoking cigars in order to obtain a box. To reduce the temptation to "light up a stogy", and to protect your health (and those around you as well), we suggest a shoebox as an alternative. However, you will have to make your own measurements, using this project as a layout guide.

There are five steps in making the set:

1) collecting all the components for the set prior to beginning construction (see the list of parts and sources at the end of this article)
2) marking the cigar box for mounting the components and drilling mounting holes
3) mounting the components on the inside and outside of the cigar box
4) wiring the component terminals together inside the box with hookup wire and solder
5) and winding the coil on the outside of the box

Step 1: Collecting the Parts. You'll note from the list of parts that you can purchase all but the variable capacitor, the high-impedance headphones, and the cigar box at a full line Radio Shack. None of the components are critical, and feel free to substitute for any of the connectors. Make sure you use a germanium diode and not a 1N914 if you substitute for the 1N34, and make sure you use a high-impedance headphone, not an 8-ohm speaker or 8-ohm earplug. If you wish to substitute a crystal earplug (about 10K ohms) in place of the high-Z headphones, add a 47 K resistor in parallel with the earplug leads.

Overview of Construction. Figures 1 and 2 denote placement of the headphone jacks, optional external antenna and ground jacks, the variable tuning knob and capacitor, and the rubber feet. Note that the bottom of the cigar box becomes the front of the radio and the right side of the cigar box when viewed normally - when lifting the lid and looking inside - becomes the bottom of the radio (with rubber feet, see Figure 2).

Step 2: Marking the cigar box for mounting the components and drilling mounting holes.

You'll need to mount four components: the optional antenna and ground jack, the headphone jacks (one piece), the variable capacitor with knob, and the 1N34 diode. While placement is not critical, make sure that you mount all components in the bottom half of the box, and tuck the optional antenna and ground jack towards the lid. This will leave room to wind the coil, and keep the box steady.

Mount the antenna and ground jack about an inch above the right side of the box and do the same for the headphone jack. Eyeball the points where the jack components will go "into" the box and then drill appropriate holes. Then place the components on the box and mark and drill the additional holes for the nuts and bolts to mount these jacks. [We don't give you any more guidelines than this since it is likely that you'll use whatever jacks you may have in your junk box anyway.] Then locate and drill holes for the variable capacitor. Make sure that the tuning shaft will come through the bottom of the box (the front of the radio when it is complete). See Figure 2 for one way of placing the variable 365 μμfd capacitor assembly.

Step 3: Mounting the components on the inside and outside of the cigar box. Once you are satisfied with the holes for the connections and the mounting nuts and bolts, go ahead and mount these components. Use glue too if necessary.

Step 4: Wiring the terminals together inside the box with hookup wire and solder.

You are now ready to add just three wires to connect the inside-the-box portion of your cigar box crystal radio. You can wire the connections by looking at the schematic (Figure 4), the Layout Diagram (Figure 2), or both. To assist, we've labeled the terminals in both the schematic and the layout diagram with corresponding letters: G (ground connections), A (antenna connections), and K (diode connections). The following steps assume that you'll wire the set by looking at Figure 2, the layout.

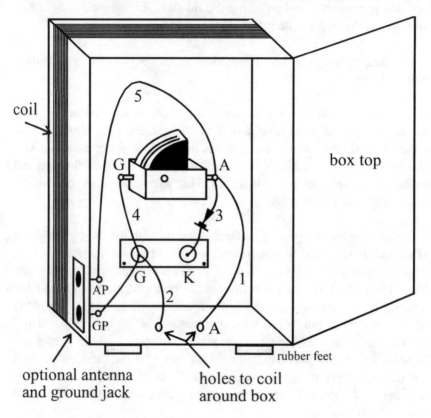

Figure 2: Back of Crystal Radio Set

a. Strip the ends of three six inch wires and attach them to the terminals as follows:

1) wire one from the headphone jack ground terminal (G) to the ground terminal of the variable capacitor,

2) wire another one from the headphone jack ground terminal (GP) to the ground terminal of the optional ground jack - to the left in the diagram,

3) wire a third from the variable capacitor (A) to the antenna terminal of the optional antenna jack (AP).

b. Attach the detector diode (probably a 1N34) between the tuning shaft terminal of the variable capacitor (A) and the positive terminal of the headphone jacks (K). Extend the leads of the diode if necessary with wire.

Step 5: Winding the coil on the outside of the box.

Once you've checked your wiring inside the cigar box, punch or drill a hole in the bottom of the radio (same side as the rubber feet) one-half inch to one side of the middle. (See Figure 3.) The coil will be wound around the edges of the box, not around the top and bottom (Figure 2).

The loop itself is made up of roughly 23 turns of #24 gauge enameled covered wire. Clean the end of the enameled wire so that the bare metal shows, and then thread the end through the hole into the inside of the cigar box. Attach the end to the negative (black) posts solder lug (G), and solder it securely. Once the solder has cooled, you may begin to wind the wire clockwise.

To make the winding of the loop more consistent, place marks on the box where the first loop should lay. You should also apply a small amount of "super glue" to the wire at each corner in order to hold it in place. You may wish to substitute double-sided carpet tape if you are working with children. Simply place the tape around the edge of the box, then wind the wire over it, and the sticky surface will hold the wire securely. (You may wish to reduce the width of the tape by cutting it in half as only a small part of the box's edge is actually covered).

If you wish for the set to have greater sensitivity and selectivity you may wish to add taps on the loop antenna, though this will add to the difficulty of construction. One benefit of this addition will be the ability to tune into the lower shortwave and possibly hear foreign broadcasts within those frequencies.

Once you have reached the 23rd or 24th turn and can reach the original entry hole at the bottom of the set, measure out an extra 6 to 8 inches, and then cut the wire from the spool. Having secured the last loop so that it will not unwind (this may be done by gluing the wire to the last corner that it rests on) proceed to drill a second entry hole in the bottom of the box on the opposite side from the original and away from the loop coil (see Figure 3). Place the loose end of the wire into box through the hole, and measure to its connection point on the stator (A), ensuring that it is neither too tight nor loose then cut off the excess. Remove the wire from the box, and then scrape the end of the wire. Place the wire back into the box and attach it to the positive (fixed stator) side of the variable capacitor (A), as shown in Figure 2. At this time, do not solder the wire, but first test the set and tune the loop antenna for optimal performance, as is explained next.

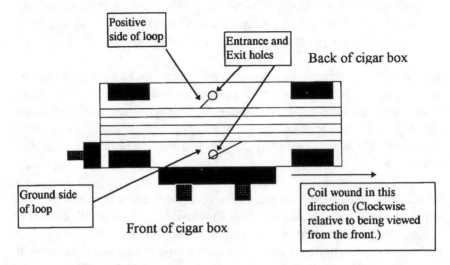

Figure 3: Bottom of Crystal Radio Set

Attach either a set of high impedance headphones, or an audio amplifier to their posts. Listen for stations by turning the variable capacitor. You should check to see if you are able to receive across the entire Standard Broadcast Band from 535 Khz to 1600 Khz, depending upon the capacitance value of your variable capacitor. Remember that you may have to "point" the set in the direction of a station in order to hear it, due to the directional nature of the loop. Once you have established that the set is working, you can then begin to tune the loop.

To first establish if your loop is out of tune, place the variable capacitor off of a station and listen to the background noise. If the loop is not tuned then you will hear a mix of different stations at all times because an out of tune loop is broad banded by nature. What you will find is that once you have tuned the loop to its proper inductance for working with the variable capacitor used, the selectivity of the loop will be greatly improved. At that point received stations will be louder, and you will hear no "ghost" stations in between. Likewise the set will become much "quieter" in its operation, which will allow you to receive stations from farther away.

To tune the loop simply unwind one loop. Do not cut it, but simply reattach the wire to the capacitor. Listen to the results, and if there is a real improvement then cut off the excessive length, clean the end, and then remove a further loop. Using a strong local station as your test, tune to that stations frequency and around it and check to see if you hear an improvement in signal. Be certain to check to see if the "ghost stations" are being reduced in volume (if not disappearing as well) and also check in the upper and lower ranges of the BCB in order to ensure that you are not losing the range of frequencies that you can bring in.

When you find that the removal of a loop will not improve the signals, and in fact these signals become weaker, add back the removed loop. At this point you can solder the loose end of the loop onto the variable capacitor (A), which ends the main construction steps.

Once the main work has been completed on the set, all that is required are a few finishing touches to personalize the set. Rubber feet, while not totally necessary, do help prevent accidental damage to the loop wire at the bottom of the set. Likewise you may wish to cover the loop wire with PVC tape in order to both protect it and improve the appearance of the set. A tuning dial made of either clear plastic or paper also adds to the look of the set.

When using the set, remember to use the directional ability of the loop by turning the set in different directions as you tune across the frequencies. Remember that even if you do not hear a station on one frequency, and in one direction, on one particular day, this does not mean that you will not hear something on another. Be certain to try tilting the set from one side to the other when listening to a station in order to hear any changes in the polarity of the radio wave front. In general, vertical radio waves tend to tilt sideways as they move away from their transmitter tower, particularly if they are traveling over earth terrain.

Another phenomenon that you can experiment with is the difference between a groundwave and a skywave. The former comes directly from the transmitting antenna, and moves along the ground as a front, while the latter is the signal that is reflected back from the ionosphere (remember that this only occurs after sundown in the broadcast band frequencies). You can tune into the skywave by tilting the set on a 45 degree angle after having tuned in a distant station, particularly if you hear a "flutter" in the signal that is characteristic of skywave. You should hear the flutter decrease, and the signal improve. Likewise you should also be able to receive more distant stations at this angle as you capture "skip" signals that are bouncing off the ionosphere and back to earth, often many hundreds of miles from their origin. Try different locations, for the travel of radio waves over land and water can have very different characteristics, and likewise the time of year can also strongly affect reception and radio wave propagation.

Parts List		Suggested source
1	Cigar box 5 1/2" X 9" X 2 1/2"	See article
1	365 pfd. variable capacitor	Xtal Set Society
1	1N34A germanium diode	RS 276-1123
1	80 ft roll of # 26 enameled wire	RS 278-1345
1	large headphone post	RS 274-632
1	small headphone post	RS 274-621
1	tuning knob	RS 274-407
4	rubber feet	RS 64-8024
1	high impedance headset	Midco
Misc.	PVC tape, solder, hook-up wire	
Midco PO Box 2288, Hollywood, FL 33022; RS=Radio Shack		

Bibliography

Cooke, B.W. "Radio Wave Radiation and Antennas" Applied Practical Radio-Television, Coyne Radio School 1947

Kendall, Jr. Lewis F. and Koehler, Robert Philip "Amplifiers, Speakers and Loops" <u>Radio Simplified : What it is—How to Build and Operate the Apparatus.</u> The John C. Winston Company 1925

Jordan, Edward C. "Electromagnetic Waves" <u>Fundamentals of Radio.</u> Prentice-Hall Inc. 1942

Trauffer, Arthur "Loop Crystal Set" <u>Radio and TV Experimenter.</u> Volume 2 1952

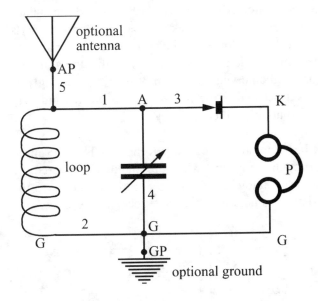

Figure 4: Circuit Diagram

A J-FET Shortwave Regenerative Receiver
By George Trudeau, NU1X, Sandwich, MA

The first general coverage receiver I ever owned was a Lafayette ExplorAir that I built from a kit. It was regenerative with 3 tubes, though one was a rectifier, and covered broadcast through 30 MHz, then called mc. I eventually graduated to a superheterodyne, then a succession of more and more complex receivers. Great performers, but I've never even opened the case of my current one. It just wasn't the same until I realized that I could still build one!

My first radio project in decades was the Quaker Oat box crystal radio project from the Xtal Set Society web page. I built it during a power outage and soldered the connections by heating an old soldering iron on my gas stove -- that somehow made it a more credible project. Payoff was when I showed it to some people at work and they couldn't conceive that it was a receiver. One summed it up best with "I see wire, I see headphones, but where's the radio?"

I decided the next step ought to be a one tube grid leak or regenerative receiver. I started looking at circuits in various old books and magazines I've accumulated through the years. A quick perusal of a current parts catalog convinced me that they no longer make coils, variable capacitors, tubes, 45 volt batteries, high voltage capacitors, or audio transformers unless there's at least one 600 ohm winding. Even something seemingly as common as a tube socket seemed to be nearly impossible to find. My basement is well stocked, but not well enough.

It was starting to look like I could duplicate my Kenwood TS-140S more easily. I had nearly forgotten the project when the mailman delivered the latest Lindsay Publications catalog and right there in the catalog was the schematic for a 3 transistor regenerative shortwave receiver.

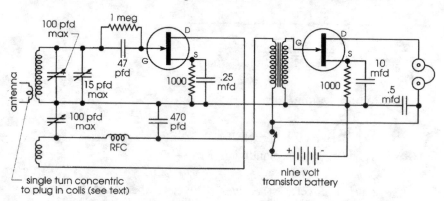

Figure 1: Solid State Equivalent of Classic "Doerle" Regenerative Receiver From the 1930's (printed by permission of Lindsay Publications)

I looked it over and said, "hey, they've got MPF-102 transistors at Radio Shack!" It wasn't going to be easy, but I found the key. My problem was that I was trying to make an antique radio when I really wanted to make a simple one.

I exchanged a few e-mail messages with Lindsay about the circuit: Q. How many turns on the coil? A. As many as you need to make it work on the band you want. Q. What's that audio transformer? A. I got it at a flea market, probably 3 to 1. Q. I built it and it's completely dead! A. Buy C. F. "Rock" Rockey's "Secrets of Homebuilt Regenerative Receivers" book. Well, that's why the circuit was in the catalog in the first place -- to get me to buy the book. It turned out to be a very well spent $9.95. The book looks small, but is absolutely loaded with information. It starts out with the history of detectors leading up to the invention of the regenerative circuit by Edwin Armstrong in 1912. It then goes on to explain how they work and why they are so sensitive and selective.

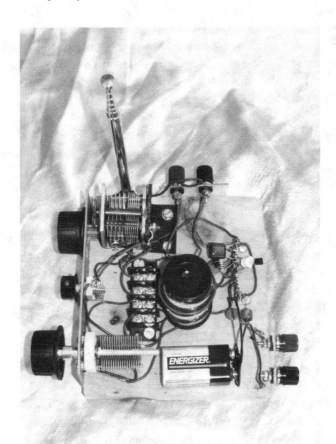

Photo #1: George's Shortwave Regen

Part 3 of the book, "Challenges of Regenerative Receiver Design," goes through the circuit component by component. It shows what component values are critical and how to select them. Finally Part 4, "Building a Practical Regenerative Receiver," covers the circuit again. This time from the perspective of actually building it. It goes through mechanical stability, phones or speakers, field effect transistors or tubes, and through nearly every detail of the design. The one thing the book doesn't have is a lot of receiver plans. There are quite a few sample circuits in the appendix, but just a couple in the main text.

I decided to rebuild my receiver. Using the book as a guide I turned the solid state version of the "Doerle" regenerative receiver on page 85 of the book into a working set. The circuit in the book is a regenerative detector stage followed by a stage of audio amplification. I decided to start out with just the detector, so I connected a pair of 2000 ohm headphones where the primary of the audio transformer is shown in the diagram. I used my dipper to make sure that the coil was on the right band—Rock's coil design data put me right on frequency—6 to 12 MHz in my case.

When I realized I had made the last connection, I hooked up the phones and battery, connected an antenna and nearly fell off my chair when I heard stations from one end of the dial to the other! The most amazing thing is how well it separates the 5 KHz spaced world band stations. I disconnected the antenna, and I could still hear stations.

It's ugly, but the people at work knew it was a radio this time. Not because it looked like one, but because they could put on the headphones and hear Radio Canada for themselves. They still think I'm nuts though. "Why don't you just buy one?" It doesn't tune quite fine enough for SSB, but the next version of it will. You see, I picked up this really neat vernier at the last flea market....

MEMBERSHIP CORRESPONDENCE

John Bailey, Springfield, OH. In response to reader Simpson's letter in Vol 7 #5, about US Broadcast reference books, he might consider:
♦"Highway Radio" 4th Ed. By William J. Stank (State by State partial listing of AM & FM stations), also alphabetical by call sign.
♦ "FM Atlas", 16th Ed., by Bruce F. Elving ("complete" listings by state and by frequency)

• "World Radio and TV Handbook", (Yearly). (Partial, 5KW & up, listings by frequency of MW AM stations of the world). [Editor. Thanks John! We will look into carrying these great references. They are currently available from Universal Radio 6830 Americana Pkwy, Reynoldsburg, OH 43068. 1-614-866-4267.]

Editor. One of our members commented that we had a short across the earphone in schematic 1 of issue number #37. Although we sometimes mix up the old conventions (we admit it) we try to stay true to the 1920's style diagrams. Modern day schematics denote a connection (short) on crossed lines with a dark dot. If the dot is missing, then the lines are not connected. Early schematics often assumed that a short existed between two crossing lines (no dot convention was used) and sometimes inserted a half circle in line on a line passing over another to denote that there was not a connection. It is not unusual, however, for hobbyists to mix these methods, so one must use "context" to figure out the wiring.

Ken Ladd, Minneapolis, MN. "There is a very interesting used book company up here that may be of interest to you as well as other xtal fans. They offer a free catalog, and one can make arrangements with them to do searches as well. I found their catalog and have verified that they are still going. The copy I have is about 260 pages and includes books and magazines. Their radio publications go back to 1914 or so." [Editor. We called and talked with Thomas, he started his business in college and has been running it ever since. He asks people to call or write for a catalog. Thanks again, Ken!]

Thomas J. Dady, Limited
2223 SIXTH STREET N.E.
MINNEAPOLIS, MN 55418
(612) 789-5074

Bob Pelley, Lorette, QC, Canada. "Hi! I just got your address from Lycos (internet search engine) and I must say that I like your website. You seem to be so far the best crystal place I've come across. I just came across a very unusual crystal radio that maybe the club experts can give me some help with! The flea market dealer I got it from, down the St. Lawrence River's south shore about 100 miles from Quebec City, says he got it from a gentleman who was born in 1907. This particular gentleman would be what we would call today a 'draft-dodger' because when Canada declared the draft during WWII, he headed for the hills. Apparently he had used this radio with an antenna and a steel stake in his 'hideout' to keep up to date on the war. This radio has a wooden box measuring roughly 6" long, 3 1/4" h (including two 'legs') and 3" deep. On the front it has a gold and red paper sticker with black letters covering maybe 2/3 of the facing. On the top half of the sticker it has a half-moon scale from 0-100. It says " Sky Ranger" with two lightening flashes. In the bottom right corner, on a small red triangle it looks like the following description:

SNI-DOR, Radio?????, Limited, (Radiocraft?, Radioaction?)

"The back of the radio is masonite and has two fahnstock clips on the left side for ground and antenna. There are two more on the right for the headphones. The cats-whisker deal is also on the back, slightly right of center. The following is written centered on the back.

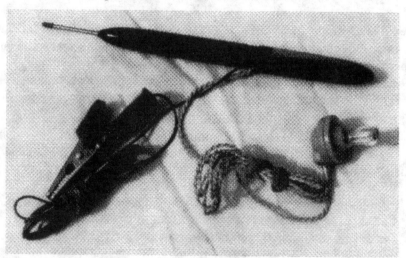

Photo #2: Spy "Pen" Radio (Johnson Smith Co.) dark blue with gold clip, slide tuning. Photo appears on page 86 of Crystal Clear, Volume 2, available from the Society. Printed here by permission of Sonoran Publishing. The Crystal Clear books include photographs of hundreds of old sets.

Model A.Y. (or maybe AV?), RAID-O-LARM, PAT. PENDING, IN EVENT OF AIR RAID WARNING, DON'T USE THE TELEPHONE, Authorities request keep line, clear for official use. COOPERATE

"The insides of the set are simple. There is a square coil which contains a round coil. Coming out of the front of the set is a shaft which turns a rod and ball along the square coil. By the way this is the first time I have ever come across a radio with a WOODEN shaft. I have heard some many years ago about a government issue or government authorized crystal radio to be used if the enemy managed to blow out the power system through an air raid, and this could be one of them. (However I don't know if it was the Cdn, US or Brit gov't). In any case, given the name of the radio 'RAID-O-LARM' and the air raid instructions, this seems to be a pretty special radio with wartime overtones. Any crystal experts out there who can give us their info or at least their speculations about this set?"

Ben Goble, Lakewood, CO. "I received a flyer in the mail from Electronics Goldmine, P.O. Box 5408, Scottsdale AZ 85261. They had AM loopstick antenna coils for $0.89 each, 10/$5.00 or 100/$40.00. These coils have four leads and a ferrite bar. They appear to be the same as the coils that are used in the Radio Shack crystal radio kits. They also advertise variable tuning caps designed to be used with the antenna coils and they run $0.99 each, 10/$6.00 or 100/$45.00. Antenna coil is part #G8538, Tuning cap is part #G8537. Electronics Goldmine order phone number is 800.445.0697. Their fax number is 602.661.8259. They also have a web page, www.goldmine-elec.com"

T.J. "Skip" Arey, Edgewater Park, NJ. "Just thought you might get a kick out of the fact that I have gone the extra mile in showing the world my devotion to the radio hobby and crystal sets in general. The basic schematic for a classic crystal set is now a permanent part of my anatomy. I had the design made into a tattoo. If you ever forget how to make a radio, just look on my right shoulder. The schematic came right from the Xtal Set Society logo as it appears on the title page and back cover of the Crystal Set Projects book. I just showed the book to the artist and he used the picture to make a five-inch stencil. It came out great. Everybody I show it to asks what it is (the most popular view is that it is an 'alien' symbol). It gives me a chance to tell them all about the radio hobby. The tattoo artist said it was the most original idea he had seen in years."

Michael "spy guy" Simpson, West Pointe, PA. [Editor. Michael wrote this story while requesting a complimentary copy of the newsletter off the internet. We get a lot of nostalgic stories in, but we thought this one was particularly great. He figured nobody would ever read it.] "When I was

11 years old, my friend and I wanted to be a secret agents. We would tail people and see what they were up to. But we needed a radio. I tried to build a radio with a battery, a speaker, and a hanger for an antenna. Obviously, it didn't work, so I asked my dad why not. He told me it was because I didn't have a 'detector'. (How many dads would know THAT?). I went to the library, and got 'The Boys Second Book of Radio and Electronics' by Alfred P. Morgan. I really didn't understand the book, but I went to an electronics store and bought a Germanium diode, a tuning capacitor, and a crystal earpiece. I made a completely untuned circuit with the Germanium diode in it, and picked up every station in the Philadelphia area, all at the same time.

"That was it. My life was completely changed. All it took was a coil of wire to make my next set work, and I was forever hooked on radio, electronics, and later, computers. I now maintain computers for the phone company, and I still build and collect crystal radios. By the way, why did we want to be secret agents? Because we liked the TV show 'Get Smart'. So you see, a crystal radio forever altered my life, and I am forever indebted to Don Adams, Alfred P. Morgan, and all the pioneers of early radio who made the miracle of communications over the airwaves possible."

RADIO BUILDING CONTEST

We would like your input and ideas as we are in the planning and development process for the next radio contest. The winners will be printed in the next book published by the Society. Along with more complicated crystal set projects, we would also like to include a few of each of the following: grid-leak, TRF, reflex, regenerative, and super-regenerative sets. Again, we will have to include 3 or so basic projects at the front for the beginner, but that doesn't mean we can't include more complicated sets in the rest of the book. How can you increase your chances of winning? Include detailed, step-by-step directions with plenty of drawings and a photograph of the finished product. The project deadline is April 15th! The prize will be $50 and 5 copies of the book for each winning article, and you may submit as many articles as you like.

THE XTAL SET SOCIETY

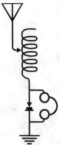

The Xtal Set Society *Newsletter*, six issues, one year subscription. (postage is included, no additional shipping charge)

$ 10.95

International subscriptions please remit US$17.00, Canadians please remit US$12.00.

Volume I & II of the Society Newsletter, twelve issues, May, 1991 through May 1993.

$ 21.90

The Crystal Set Handbook and Volume III of the Society Newsletter, three issues, ending Nov. 1993.

$ 11.95

Volume IV of the Society Newsletter, six issues, ending November 1994.

$ 10.95

Crystal Sets: Volume V of the Society Newsletter, six issues, ending November 1995.

$ 10.95

Crystal Set Building and More: Volume 6 & 7 of the Society Newsletter, ending November 1998.

$ 15.95

Crystal Radio: History, Fundamentals, and Design
By P.A Kinzie

$ 11.95

Crystal Set Projects: 15 Radio Projects You Can Build
New book! Written by members of the Society, 1997

$ 14.95

Shipping and handling on book orders

$ 3.95

Only $2.50 no matter how many books you order. International orders $6 shipping per book, or write for exact amount. MO residents add 5.975% sales tax.

The Xtal Set Society
e-mail: xtalset@midnightscience.com
www.midnightscience.com
1-800-927-1771

THE CRYSTAL SET HANDBOOK

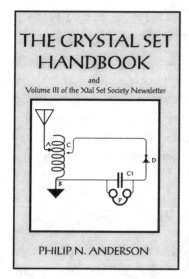

THE CRYSTAL SET HANDBOOK
and
Volume III of the Xtal Set Society Newsletter

PHILIP N. ANDERSON

There is nothing else like this handbook. It takes the reader beyond the basics and discusses the math and mechanisms behind the mystery of the crystal set. "This book is written for crystal set enthusiasts, radio amateurs, first-time radio experimenters, and electronics students. I wrote it to encourage design, building, and experimentation" —Phil Anderson. Contents of the book include an introduction to the crystal set with a simple oat box project, formulas for coil inductance and coil Q, a procedure for measuring coil capacitance, introductory and advanced chapters on L-C circuit matching, and Volume III of the Xtal Set Society Newsletter (3 issues). 8x5½ paperback, pgs 133. $11.95

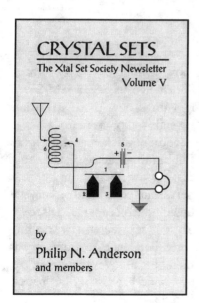

CRYSTAL SETS
The Xtal Set Society Newsletter
Volume V

by
Philip N. Anderson
and members

CRYSTAL SETS:VOLUME V

Volume V of the Society newsletter includes six issues ending November 1995. Great for new members to get current, those wanting a bound copy for their reference bookshelf, or as a gift to get a friend started. Contents include: The Design of Unpowered AM Receivers, Radio Outfit in a Headset, A Crystal Set Revisited-Reconstructed, Grounded Loopstick Tuner, The Matching Secret, and lots of membership correspondence. 8½ x 5½ paperback. $10.95

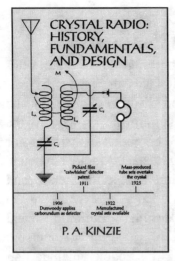

CRYSTAL RADIO: HISTORY, FUNDAMENTALS, & DESIGN

Written by a long-time member of the Xtal Set Society, Mr. Phil Kinzie, this book chronicles the fascinating history and development of the crystal detector. Starting with the discovery of solid-state rectification and then through the development of the crystal detector, the reader learns about great inventors such as Pickard, Braun, Dunwoody, and others. Radio fundamentals such as antennas, ground, lightning protection, tuned circuits, and detection are covered for the beginner. The unending compromise between selectivity and sensitivity is discussed for the crystal set designer. Advanced topics such as the use of multi-tuned circuits and wave traps follow for the serious experimenter. 8½ x 5½ paperback, 124 pages. $11.95

CRYSTAL SET LOOPERS
A 3 TUBER & MORE: *New!*

Volume 8 of the Society Newsletter is now available as a paperback book. It's the best volume yet! Build a Shortwave looper, a AM/SW 3 tuber, a Antenna Tuner/AM Trap, a Loop with a new twist, a Frisbee

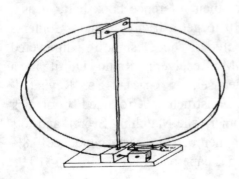

crystal radio, a radio from a deodorant stick, and find more fun building ideas. Learn about biasing effects on diode performance and crystal detector experiments. Discover crystal set secrets by reading correspondence from our members all over the world. 6 x 9 paperback, 128 pages. **$15.95**

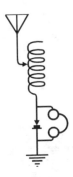

VOLUME IV Great stuff from 1994, includes hints on measuring coil capacitance, two building projects using Quaker Oats boxes, broadcast and short-wave, how to make home-brew headphones and curve tracers, how crystal earphones work, and a description and schematic of 10 crystal sets. 8½ x 5½ paperback, 85 pages. $10.95

Crystal Set Projects: 15 Radio Projects You Can Build

Crystal Set Projects is a collection of radio projects that won a recent building contest run by the Society. Thanks to everyone who participated. If you missed out, don't worry. We're doing another! Included are step-by-step instructions so you can build and design your own Xtal sets no matter what your background in electronics. The projects are of various designs and difficulty so that everyone can learn something. "Crystal set circuits have been regularly published in the hobby press since the dawn of radio. But the Xtal Set Society's new project book covers more electronic and mechanical variations of this ever-popular receiver than I have ever seen in one place. You'll find hi tech and low tech versions, vintage and modern versions, sets with loop antennas and short-wave bands. The book is as much fun to read as to build from, but I defy anyone to browse this infectious publication for long without experiencing an uncontrollable urge to break out the soldering iron and double-cotton-covered wire!" —Marc Ellis, Editor, The Old-Timer's Bulletin of the AWA; Contributing Editor, Antique Radio, Popular Electronics magazine. Get yourself a copy! 6 x 9 paperback, 160 pages, $14.95.

The Xtal Set Society is dedicated to once again building and experimenting with radio electronics, often—but not always—through the use of the crystal set, the basis for most modern day radio apparatus. The Society newsletter helps support our goal of producing excellent quality technical books that encourage learning and building. To join the society and receive one year (6 issues) of the bi-monthly newsletter, remit $12.95 to The Xtal Set Society. Canadians, please remit US $14.00. Outside the US and Canada please remit US $19.00. Thank You!

The Xtal Set Society
P.O. Box 3026, St. Louis, MO 63130
(314) 725-1172; (314) 725-7062 fax; 1-800-927-1771 VISA/MC
e-mail: xtalset@midnightscience.com
www.midnightscience.com

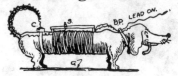